CANADIAN GOLD

2010 Olympic Winter Games Ice Hockey Champions

CANADA

® Registered trademark of Hockey Canada
® Marque déposée de Hockey Canada

Officially licensed product
of Hockey Canada.

Produit officiellement licencié
de Hockey Canada.

The Team Canada logo is a registered
trademark of Hockey Canada and
is used under license by Fenn
Publishing Company Ltd.

Le logo d'Équipe Canada est une marque
déposée de Hockey Canada et utilisée sous
licence par Fenn Publishing Company Ltd.

Official licensed product of the Canadian
Olympic Committee.

The COC logo is a registered trademark
of the Canadian Olympic Committee and
used under license by Fenn Publishing
Company Ltd. All rights reserved.

Ⓜ Official Mark of the Canadian Olympic Committee
Marque officielle du Comité olympique canadien

Fenn Publishing Company Ltd.

CANADIAN GOLD

2010 Olympic Winter Games Ice Hockey Champions

A Fenn Publishing Book / First Published in 2010
All rights reserved
Text Copyright © Andrew Podnieks
Copyright © Hockey Canada
Copyright © Canadian Olympic Committee

The publisher gratefully acknowledges the support of the Canada Council for the Arts
and the Ontario Arts Council for its publishing program. We acknowledge the support
of the Government of Ontario through the Ontario Media Development Corporation's
Ontario Book Initiative.

THE CANADA COUNCIL | LE CONSEIL DES ARTS
FOR THE ARTS | DU CANADA
SINCE 1957 | DEPUIS 1957

ONTARIO ARTS COUNCIL
CONSEIL DES ARTS DE L'ONTARIO

We acknowledge the financial support of the Government of Canada through the
Book Publishing Industry Development Program (BPIDP) for our publishing activities.

Designed by First Image

Fenn Publishing Company Ltd.
Toronto, Ontario, Canada

Printed in Canada

Library and Archives Canada Cataloguing in Publication
Podnieks, Andrew
    Canadian gold / Andrew Podnieks.
ISBN 978-1-55168-384-3
1. Winter Olympic Games (21st : 2010 : Vancouver, B.C.).
2. Hockey--Canada--History--21st century. I. Title.
GV848.4.C3P643 2010   796.962'66   C2010-901104-X

CANADIAN GOLD

2010 Olympic Winter Games Ice Hockey Champions

ANDREW PODNIEKS

Fenn Publishing Company Ltd.
Toronto, Canada

CONTENTS

FOREWORD

Playing hockey for Canada is the greatest—and most challenging—thrill a hockey player can experience. It's the greatest because representing your country is the pinnacle of a player's career. It's the most challenging, though, because in Canada fans expect to win gold every time their team puts on the maple leaf sweater.

Coming into Vancouver 2010, everybody expected Canada to win gold in both the men's and women's tournaments. At Hockey Canada, we did all we could to provide the players every opportunity to realize their dreams, and now we can celebrate this double victory.

Team Canada has done it!

Although winning Olympic gold is the greatest achievement a player can hope to attain, it is not a victory that happens over just two weeks while the games are played. Victory starts at the grassroots level, where more than 600,000 boys and girls play the game for fun. In the arenas across the country, in the driveways on our streets, wherever you can run or skate with a stick and puck or ball, that's where our Olympians come from.

And these 600,000 kids owe everything they have to their moms and dads, to the volunteers and organizers who help youngsters get equipment, learn the game, and develop a lifelong love of the game.

Of course, the wins here in Vancouver are the result of this dedication coming to the highest levels for the most important international tournament of the players' lives. The men and women of Team Canada will never get a chance to play in another Olympics on home ice, never get to hear the roar of the incredible home crowds or walk down the streets and feel the support they had in Vancouver.

The players and management of the men's and women's national teams that won gold here deserve all the credit in the world for their dedication to being the best and playing their best, both as individuals and as members of their respective teams.

Today is a day we can all be proud to be Canadian. Congratulations to our national men's and women's hockey teams—Olympic champions for 2010.

Bob Nicholson
President, Hockey Canada

INTRODUCTION

The entire country shut down on Sunday, February 28, 2010, at 12:30 p.m. Pacific time when Canada and the United States faced off for the gold medal in men's hockey to end the Vancouver Olympics.

Two-and-a-half hours later, when Sidney Crosby scored the overtime goal at 7:40, the historic showdown immediately defined glory for this generation. For the rest of our lives, we will talk about "where we were" when Crosby one-timed Jarome Iginla's pass for the 3–2 victory.

It was not an easy gold medal. It feels like a century ago now, but it all began when Hockey Canada president Bob Nicholson named Steve Yzerman the executive director for these Olympics. Yzerman then selected his coaching staff, choosing the man he knew and trusted the most, Mike Babcock. They have worked together with the Detroit Red Wings, and the fit was a natural one.

If that was a difficult process, choosing the 23 players for the team was an agonizing one. But when the roster was finally announced, the pressure and scrutiny began in earnest. It is absolutely certain that no team has ever faced the intense expectations that these 23 players faced from the day they got the call to represent their country to the day they won gold. Everyone made it clear that gold was the only result that would be acceptable. Silver or bronze were simply the colours of failure.

For the women's team, the challenge was equally pronounced. While Canada has played in every gold-medal game at the Olympics and World Championships, the nation has not always defeated its arch-rival, the United States. However, coach Melody Davidson put together a roster deep in talent and experience, and these qualities took the team to gold on February 25, 2010. Although the veterans were vital to the win, it was the brilliant play of young goalie Shannon Szabados and the two goals from Marie-Philip Poulin that carried the day.

Then, three days later, Crosby scored the goal of the 21st century, and the country rejoiced. Another double gold for the home of hockey. Canada—Olympic champions again.

—Andrew Podnieks

MEN'S EXECUTIVE

The building of an Olympic hockey team is a process with many stages, but it all begins with the naming of the executive staff in charge of everything Olympic. On October 18, 2008, Bob Nicholson, president and CEO of Hockey Canada, named the four men who would oversee the team for Vancouver 2010, starting with Steve Yzerman as executive director. Assisting him was Kevin Lowe, president of the Edmonton Oilers and a member of the staff in 2002 and 2006; Ken Holland, the executive vice-president and general manager of the Detroit Red Wings; and Doug Armstrong, assistant general manager of the St. Louis Blues.

"Hockey Canada is going to Vancouver to make all Canadians proud in 2010, and Steve is just the person to lead us," Nicholson said during the press conference to introduce the team. "Steve is well respected throughout the hockey world for good reason. He has served this country whenever called upon, and we are thrilled that he will be leading our Men's Olympic Team in 2010."

Almost since the day he retired in 2006, Yzerman has remained with the Red Wings as vice-president, learning the business side of hockey from Holland. Yzerman acted as Team Canada's general manager for both the 2007 and 2008 World Championships, and, of course, his extraordinary Hall-of-Fame career as a player gave him valuable on-ice experience, preparing him for just such a prominent role with Hockey Canada.

"I am truly honoured and privileged to take on the role of executive director for Hockey Canada going into 2010," Yzerman said. "I am also very excited about the group that we have in place, a group that has great experience at both the professional and international level. With support from Bob Nicholson, Johnny Misley, and the Hockey Canada team, I know that we have the right mix in place to assemble a team that will make all Canadians proud in 2010."

The next stage was for the executive team to put together a coaching staff. Given the sheer number of candidates, this proved to be a time-consuming and thought-provoking endeavour. On June 25, 2009, Yzerman introduced his own Mike Babcock of the Red Wings as Canada's coach. Babcock would be supported by assistants Lindy Ruff, Ken Hitchcock, and Jacques Lemaire.

Babcock had coached Canada's juniors to victory in 1997, and the senior team to gold at the 2004 World Championship. He also led Detroit to the Stanley Cup in 2008, and to the finals a year later. Winning Gold in Vancouver has made him the first coach to win all Triple Gold Club honours. Ruff and Hitchcock had both coached Canada at the two most recent World Championships, Hitchcock in Quebec City in 2008, and Ruff in Switzerland last year. Lemaire had no previous experience with international hockey, but his Hall-of-Fame credentials as a player with the Montreal Canadiens were impeccable.

"With Canada's great passion for hockey, we are lucky to be able to count on a long list of quality Canadian coaches, which gave the management group many great options," Yzerman noted at the time he introduced the men behind the bench. "As a group, we are very pleased with the coaching staff that we have announced today, a group with extensive international and professional experience and success. We look forward to the challenge ahead and are proud to represent Canada in Vancouver in February."

Once the entire team was in place, that left two key dates on the Hockey Canada calendar. The men held a four-day orientation camp in Calgary last August, when 46 players (or, two full teams) were invited to meet, discuss every detail about the Olympics, and skate together under the watchful eyes of coaches for the only time as a group. Then, on December 30, 2009, at the World Junior (U20) Championship in Saskatoon, Yzerman took to the stage for the most important press conference before the Olympics to announce Team Canada's players. After that, it was a matter of keeping fingers crossed in the hopes none of the three goalies, seven defencemen, or 13 forwards suffered an injury prior to the first game in Vancouver on February 16, 2010 while waiting to play in Vancouver.

Melody Davidson has been coaching Team Canada's women on and off for some 16 years, starting as an assistant coach with the 1994 World Women's Championship. Her commitment to the program and Hockey Canada's respect for her abilities reached new levels on May 17, 2006. She signed a four-year contract as the first full-time general manager (and head coach) for the women's programs.

In order to assume this full-time position, Davidson resigned as head coach of Cornell University, where she had been for three seasons. The signing came after leading the team to Gold at the 2006 Olympics in Turin. Davidson followed up with another win at the 2007 World Women's Championship.

Soon after, Davidson resigned as coach to focus on her role as general manager, but after Peter Smith led the team to a disappointing silver medal at the 2008 WWC, Davidson took over the head coaching position again. Smith and Doug Lidster were her assistants in Vancouver.

The potential players for Vancouver had a busy summer. They first met in Dawson Creek, British Columbia from May 25 to June 17, 2009, for what was billed as a conditioning camp. Of course, in addition to identifying every player's strengths and weaknesses, it was also a great opportunity for the players to get to know each other better.

The coaching staff brought all 26 players together last August in Calgary as the next step toward announcing the women's roster on December 21, 2009. The team could take 21 players, so, in the coming months, five players had to be cut.

Team Canada had been centralizing since 2005, and this was the second year that the team played midget AAA boys teams in Alberta in preparation for Vancouver 2010. In all, the women had a record of 16–10. Additionally, they played the United States ten times, winning seven games, giving the team added confidence heading to the Olympics.

"The NWT Midget Series was a great way to showcase the strength of the women's game and gave fans across Alberta the chance to see some of the top players in the world," said Davidson. "The games we played against AAA Midget teams also provided us with on-ice situations that couldn't be replicated in our practices. And as a result we leave for Vancouver prepared and confident."

The first cuts came on November 25, 2009, when Davidson sent home Brianne Jenner and Jocelyne Larocque. Two weeks later, Delaney Collins, a veteran of five WWC events, was cut. Two more players were cut the day before the roster was announced—Gillian Ferrari, another veteran, and youngster Jennifer Wakefield. The next day, the roster for Vancouver was set.

"It was tough, really difficult," Davidson said about cutting Ferrari. "Gillian has a lot of connections to the team, so it was tough for the team as well. It was close. We had the seven [defencemen]. In the end, we felt the D [defencemen] we kept were a little more mobile. That was really it."

The final team continued to play in the midget series, and the final event for the team came from February 1–6, 2010. The players spent a week in Jasper, Alberta training together for the final time before the first game. The entire women's team arrived in Vancouver on February 11, prepared for a fight to win its third straight Olympic Gold.

Saturday, February 13, 2010

Yesterday, speed skater Clara Hughes was the flag-bearer for Canada at the Opening Ceremony for the 2010 Olympic Winter Games in Vancouver. The women's hockey team marched into B.C. Place, but the men were still playing in the NHL. Later in the evening, Canada's captain, Hayley Wickenheiser, took the Olympic oath on behalf of all athletes: "In the name of all the competitors, I promise that we shall take part in these Olympic Games, respecting and abiding by the rules which govern them, committing ourselves to a sport without doping and without drugs, in the true spirit of sportsmanship, for the glory of sport and the honour of our teams."

WOMEN'S HOCKEY

Canada began its defence of Olympic Gold with a crushing and record-setting victory over Slovakia, a country which qualified for Vancouver a year and a half ago in stunning fashion. The Slovaks, who had hammered Bulgaria 82–0 in the pre-qualification game in September 2008, were on the receiving end of a lopsided score before 16,496 screaming pro-Canadian fans. Jayna Hefford had a hat trick and three assists, Meghan Agosta had a hat trick and two assists, and Caroline Ouellette had a goal and four assists. Of Canada's 18 skaters, only Meaghan Mikkelson failed to record at least one point.

First Period

After spending the first several seconds in their own end, the Canadians stormed down the ice and didn't leave until 1:39 when they scored the opening goal to thunderous applause before the wildly partisan crowd. Not surprisingly, Haley got the goal, but it was Irwin, not Wickenheiser this time. This despite three brilliant saves by Slovakian goalie Zuzana Tomcikova to keep the game goalless for the first 99 seconds.

Meghan Agosta got goal number two on a delayed penalty at 3:06 when she deftly deflected Tessa Bonhomme's point shot. She got her second and the team's third on a power play less than three minutes later, beating the helpless Tomcikova with a great wrist shot over the glove.

Carla MacLeod deflected another Bonhomme point shot during a 4-on-4 which found its way through a maze of players and through the legs of Tomcikova. Canada made it 5–0 on a strange play. Agosta was dragged down, splitting the defence, and while the referee was signaling a penalty Michaela Matejova seemed to touch the puck. At the same time, Jayna Hefford swatted at the puck and Matejova's stick, the puck fooled Tomcikova for the goal.

Gina Kingsbury made it an even half dozen after taking a great Gillian Apps pass from behind the net and roofing it over the oft-used glove of Tomcikova at 15:09. Another point shot, this from Colleen Sostorics, was inadvertently re-directed by a Slovakian for a 7–0 lead at 16:20.

Second Period

It took all of 3:42 of the second period before Sarah Vaillancourt made it 8–0 with another high shot off a nice cross-ice pass from Rebecca Johnston. Newcomer Marie-Philip Poulin got the next goal, on a power play, walking in from the corner and backhanding a shot off the post and into the net.

Wave after wave, shift after shift, attacked the Slovakian goal, and Tomcikova fought valiantly as the last—and often only—line of

PRELIMINARY ROUND

CANADA **18**

VS

SLOVAKIA **0**

CANADA HOCKEY PLACE

SATURDAY, FEBRUARY 13, 2010

GAME SUMMARY

First Period

#			Time
1.	Canada,	Irwin (Vaillancourt, Johnston)	1:39
2.	Canada,	Bonhomme (Hefford, MacLeod)	3:06
3.	Canada,	Agosta (Ouellette, Wickenheiser)	5:38
4.	Canada,	MacLeod (Bonhomme, Ouellette)	8:21
5.	Canada,	Agosta (Kellar, Sostorics)	11:34
6.	Canada,	Kingsbury (Piper, Apps)	15:09
7.	Canada,	Sostorics (Hefford, Agosta)	16:20

Penalties: Pravlikova (SVK) 4:21, Karafiatova (SVK) & Vaillancourt (CAN) 7:02, Kapustova (SVK) 8:36, Culikova (SVK) 12:48, Agosta (CAN) 19:24

Second Period

#			Time
8.	Canada,	Vaillancourt (Johnston)	3:42
9.	Canada,	Poulin (unassisted)	7:21
10.	Canada,	Agosta (Hefford, Ouellette)	10:19
11.	Canada,	Hefford (Wickenheiser)	12:00
12.	Canada,	Ouellette (Apps)	12:44
13.	Canada,	MacLeod (Poulin, Sostorics)	16:42

Penalties: Babonyova (SVK) 5:33, Irwin (CAN) 11:48

Third Period

#			Time
14.	Canada,	Hefford (Agosta, MacLeod)	4:23
15.	Canada,	Irwin (Vaillancourt, Ward)	4:37
16.	Canada,	Piper (Wickenheiser)	6:54
17.	Canada,	Hefford (Ouellette, Kellar)	11:03
18.	Canada,	Kingsbury (Botterill)	12:52

Penalties: Mikkelson (CAN) 0:51, Ward (CAN) 16:19, Pravlikova (SVK), 19:45

In Goal
Slovakia—Tomcikova
Canada—St. Pierre

Shots on Goal

Slovakia	4	2	3	9
Canada	21	25	21	67

Referee—Joy Tottman (GBR)
Linesmen—Zuzana Arazimova (CZE) & Meghan Hishmeh (USA)

Attendance: 16,496

defence. Case in point: Agosta's goal to make it 10–0, coming off a scramble in which Tomcikova made at least four stops as Canadians whacked away at the loose puck while helpless Slovakian defenders did little.

The 11–0 goal from Jayna Hefford was a thing of beauty. On a short-handed rush, Hayley Wickenheiser drove to the goal before sliding a perfect pass across the crease which Hefford merely had to re-direct into the open side of the goal.

Great work behind the Slovak goal by Gillian Apps produced the twelfth goal as she out-fought two players and got the puck in the slot where Caroline Ouellette rifled a high shot home for a 12–0 lead. This came during the same short-handed situation, and marked the first time in women's Olympic hockey history that a team had scored twice in the same opponent's power play.

Carla MacLeod made it a baker's dozen late in the period by squeezing a shot five-hole on the beleaguered Tomcikova.

Third Period

It took Canada 4:23 to make it 14–0 thanks to a fine pass by Agosta in front of the crease where Hefford one-timed the puck home. On the ensuing faceoff, it was 15–0 on a similar play, except that Irwin's pass went off a defender's skate, then between Tomcikova's pads, and in.

^ *The opening faceoff to start the 2010 Olympics women's hockey tournament, Canada against Slovakia.*

ᵛ *Gillain Apps watches at the puck slides between the pads of a sprawled goalie, Zuzana Tomcikova.*

Jayna Hefford (left) and Tessa Bonhomme celebrate one of the team's 18 goals on this record-setting day.

Cherie Piper made it 16–0 on another in-close pass, this from Wickenheiser again. This goal tied the Olympic record set by Canada in 2006 against their Italian host. Hefford's hat-trick goal at 11:03 set the record as she blew by defenceman Michaela Matejova along the left wing and slipped the puck between Tomcikova's pads as she cut across the crease.

Jennifer Botterill's great pass to Gina Kingsbury off the rush was another gem to make it 18–0 at 12:52. That's how the game ended, and as the Slovaks skated off the ice, Tomcikova received a standing ovation for her incredible effort in the face of the relentless rubber onslaught. 🍁

<Slovakian goalie Zuzana Tomcikova may have given up 18 goals, but she gets hearty congratulations from Canada's captain, Hayley Wickenheiser.*

ᵛProps all around as Canada romps to victory against a less-skilled Slovakian team.*

DAY 3

Four years of patience and hard work finally paid off for goaltender Shannon Szabados. She has played at just about every level for Team Canada in international competition, and she was named the third goalie in the last two World Women's Championships, but it wasn't until today that she was finally named the starting goalie for tomorrow's game against Switzerland. The Swiss weren't a top opponent, but the experience would give her a taste of the highest level of competition. In the end, she played the whole game and allowed one goal. Although she will have trouble unseating Kim St. Pierre and Charline Labonte from the coveted positions, Szabados seems poised to inherit the first spot that becomes available.

Sunday, February 14, 2010

CANADA

The Canadian men arrived from all corners of North America late Sunday night, but by Monday morning they were all on the ice together as a team, under the watchful eye of their coach, Mike Babcock.

Of course, the coach had many decisions to make on day one, and he surprised many of the enormous media horde by declaring that Roberto Luongo would start the first game against Norway, and two days later Martin Brodeur would start against Switzerland. The decision was wise for several reasons. First, Luongo, a member of the Vancouver Canucks, would help get the crowd behind the team right from the get-go. The move also meant a couple of precious rest days for Brodeur, the busiest goalie in the NHL. Also, Switzerland was considered a tougher opponent.

As for line combinations, Babcock started his first practice with these combinations up front: Rick Nash–Sidney Crosby–Patrice Bergeron; Eric Staal–Ryan Getzlaf–Corey Perry; the San Jose line of Patrick Marleau–Joe Thornton–Dany Heatley; and, a fourth line using three of these four—Mike Richards, Brenden Morrow, Jonathan Toews and Jarome Iginla.

Defence pairings included the Chicago Blackhawks' duo of Duncan Keith and Brent Seabrook; Chris Pronger and Dan Boyle; Scott Niedermayer (captain) and Shea Weber. Twenty-year-old Drew Doughty was the seventh man but had no reason to feel excluded.

"We think we have minutes for everyone," Babcock offered. "No one is going to play the amount of minutes they play in the National Hockey League. We've made that very clear to the group that it's not about them, it's not about me, it's about Canada. We want them all involved in the game."

WOMEN'S HOCKEY

It wasn't a record-setting 18–0 blowout like the first game, but Canada wore down Switzerland to the tune of 10–1 today at Thunderbird Arena to maintain top spot in Group A of the women's preliminary round standings. The result kept Switzerland without a win through two games. Meghan Agosta led the way with two goals, giving her five for the tournament to lead all scorers.

The Swiss, however, did win a moral victory of sorts. Darcia Leimgruber's goal with just 13.3 seconds left in the second period was the first for the Swiss women against Canada in the history of women's hockey. They had lost 6–0 in 1997, 10–0 in 1999, and 9–0 in 2007.

Shannon Szabados, frequently the third goalie in international play, made her senior debut with Team Canada.

First Period

Smaller and physically weaker, the Swiss made no pretense about the expected outcome of the game. Coach Rene Kammerer often had all five of his players adopt a strictly defensive position inside their own blue line, content merely to keep the Canadians at bay and the score down.

"We wanted to use our speed, not only by moving our feet but by moving the puck. We have a very good team that's built for transition hockey, and it's such a key component of our game," said Caroline Ouellette.

The Canadians broke the ice at 6:27 on the power play when Gina Kingsbury directed a low shot on goal which Gillian Apps deflected perfectly to the top corner.

Canada made it 2–0 eight minutes later, just moments after killing off its first penalty of the period. Rebecca Johnston came out of the penalty box, streaked down the left wing, and cut in sharply on goal. Florence Schelling stopped the shot, but Sarah Vaillancourt poked home the rebound.

Second Period

Canada made it 3–0 just 2:19 into the second period thanks to Cherie Piper. Her initial shot in the slot was blocked by a defenceman, but as Schelling moved over to make the save, Piper got the rebound and had the whole net to shoot at.

Meagan Agosta made it 4–0 on another great deflection in front, this off a Catherine Ward point shot at 8:08, and Agosta got her second of the game three minutes later on a great rush which she capped with a high backhand over Schelling's glove. It was her tournament-leading fifth goal.

"We do a lot of drills where we set up in front of the net," Ouellette said. "We have a lot of young players who can tip the puck

PRELIMINARY ROUND

CANADA   10
VS
SWITZERLAND ✚ 1

UBC THUNDERBIRD ARENA

MONDAY, FEBRUARY 15, 2010

GAME SUMMARY

First Period
1. Canada, Apps (Kingsbury, Piper) — 6:27
2. Canada, Vaillancourt (Johnston) — 14:25

Penalties: S. Marty (SUI) 5:27, Meier (SUI) 10:24, Johnston (CAN) 12:11, Nussbaum (SUI) 16:44, Kingsbury (CAN) 18:34

Second Period
3. Canada, Piper (Wickenheiser) — 2:19
4. Canada, Agosta (Ward, Ouellette) — 8:08
5. Canada, Agosta (Ouellette, Hefford) — 11:15
6. Switzerland, Leimgruber (Lehmann, S. Marty) — 19:46

Penalties: Ouellette (CAN) 15:25, Vaillancourt (CAN) 20:00

Third Period
7. Canada, Hefford (Wickenheiser) — 0:54
8. Canada, Ward (unassisted) — 9:08
9. Canada, Poulin (unassisted) — 9:27
10. Canada, Johnston (Vaillancourt, Kellar) — 10:43
11. Canada, Wickenheiser (Piper, Apps) — 11:55

Penalties: Irwin (CAN) 13:55, Nussbaum (SUI) 19:31

In Goal
Canada—Szabados
Switzerland—Schelling (51:55 L 10 GA/Slongo 8:05 nd 0 GA

Shots on Goal

Canada	16	21	25	62
Switzerland	2	7	3	12

Referee—Hertich (GER)
Linesmen—Majapuro (FIN), Rolstad (USA)

Attendance: 5,413

^Hayley Wickenheiser controls the puck while Swiss goalie Florence Schelling tries to maintain her balance and position.

ᵛ The Swiss celebrate their first ever goal against Canada in international hockey.

no matter where it's shot." Indeed, several goals against Slovakia in the opener were also the result of deflections.

Leimgruber's goal finished off a second period in which the Swiss made several confident forays into the Canadian end. Finally, as time wound down, captain Kathrin Lehmann's point shot was redirected in front over the shoulder of Szabados for the historic first goal.

"It's a very good feeling to score the first goal ever against Canada as the number-one hockey country," said Darcia Leimgruber, who scored the landmark goal for the Swiss. "Of course we're also sad that they scored ten goals against us, but at the end we have to be realistic. They're all professionals, they're all one head taller than us, so we could just give our best and enjoy the goal we scored. Now we have to beat Slovakia and then we'll see what we can reach in this tournament."

Third Period

Not too happy with the end of the second period, Canada came out with a vengeance in the final period, Jayna Hefford blowing by defenceman Stephanie Marty and beating Schelling with a great deke just 54 seconds after the puck dropped.

Goals followed quickly from Catherine Ward, Marie-Philip Poulin, Rebecca Johnston, and Hayley Wickenheiser, the nicest

^ *Jayna Hefford enjoys another goal by Team Canada against the Swiss.*

coming on a rink-long dash by Poulin who made a beautiful move around Laura Benz at top speed. The last resulted in Schelling's being pulled in favour of Dominique Slongo.

"I don't think I was tired, but I was getting there," Schelling admitted. She and Slongo faced 62 shots while Szabados had to deal with 12. "They're a top team. They're together all year while we had two camps together." ❧

Hayley Wickenheiser is checked by Switzerland's Stefanie Wyss.

Canada's women's team coach, Melody Davidson, denounced media and critics who scorned Canada's high-scoring offence that trounced its first two competitors by scores of 18–0 (Slovakia) and 10–1 (Switzerland), asserting that a double standard exists.

She noted that when the national junior team hammered opponents last month at the World Junior (U20) Championship, fans praised the teenagers for superb skill, especially after a 16–0 pasting of Latvia. But when the women run up the score, they are criticized for unsportsmanlike play. "It's a no-win situation," she said. "I think it's a double standard and it's quite unfair."

Davidson said the players "care about what Canadians and the world think of them. The goal differential is sort of secondary. It's more about playing your best. We didn't come here to put on a second-class show. We came here to play our best on any given day and hopefully win five hockey games."

They care a lot about the game," she continued. "They consider themselves leaders in the sport. It does drain them, and it drains me," Davidson said of the criticism. "They're caught between me telling them to work hard and battle and have good habits and what they have to deal with when they get off the ice."

Tuesday, February 16, 2010

MEN'S HOCKEY

PRELIMINARY ROUND

CANADA 8

VS

NORWAY 0

CANADA HOCKEY PLACE

TUESDAY, FEBRUARY 16, 2010

GAME SUMMARY

First Period
No Scoring

Penalties: Weber (CAN) 7:39, T. Jakobsen (NOR) 13:03, Spets (NOR) 17:56

Second Period
1. Canada, Iginla (Crosby, Doughty)	2:30
2. Canada, Heatley (Pronger, Thornton)	4:27
3. Canada, Richards (Bergeron, Weber)	11:06

Penalties: Hansen (NOR) 0:43, Bergeron (CAN) 7:54, Staal (CAN) 9:06, Bastiansen (NOR) 14:37, Heatley (CAN) 18:33

Third Period
4. Canada, Getzlaf (Niedermayer, Toews)	4:29
5. Canada, Heatley (Marleau, Boyle)	6:43
6. Canada, Iginla (Nash, Crosby)	7:36
7. Canada, Perry (Staal, Boyle)	11:03
8. Canada, Iginla (Crosby)	18:11

Penalties: Crosby (CAN) 1:43, T. Jakobsen (NOR) 6:13, Bastiansen (NOR) 18:57

In Goal
Canada—Luongo
Norway—Grotnes 44:29 L 4 GA/Lysenstoen 15:31 nd 4 GA

Shots on Goal
Canada	14	16	12	42
Norway	4	6	5	15

Referees—Ronn (FIN), Rooney (USA)
Linesmen—Fonselius (FIN), Nowak (USA)

Attendance: 16,652

Canada defeated Norway by an 8–0 score at Canada Hockey Place to move into a tie for first place in Group A with the United States, earlier winners against the Swiss, 3–1. Jarome Iginla led the way with three goals while linemate Sidney Crosby had three assists. Roberto Luongo made 15 saves for the shutout.

If there were a Norwegian fan among the sold-out crowd, he or she was neither visible nor audible above the din of pro-Canadian chants and cheers which reached thunderous levels when the players skated out for the opening faceoff. Never before have Crosby, Niedermayer, Nash, Thornton, Toews, Pronger, and the rest of the group played together as a team, and fans clearly appreciated this moment in hockey history.

First Period

Coach Mike Babcock decided to start local boy Roberto Luongo in goal, a smart decision if only because the Vancouver Canucks' star was cheered—and "Looooooed"—every time he touched the puck. He made the few tough saves when he had to.

The Canadians started out with all the expected energy, but the Norwegians did not play the perfect visitors by caving in. Wave after wave of Canadian attacks looked impressive. The players seemed one and all over six feet tall with energy to burn and an ability to move the puck at top speed. They did, however, show nerves around the goal of Pal Grotnes who was solid, if unspectacular, in a scoreless first period.

Coach Mike Babcock started the game with Crosby at centre between Rick Nash and Patrice Bergeron, but after only a couple of shifts he started looking for other wingers for Canada's famous number 87. Soon enough, though, they were back together.

The Norwegians were content to play stifling defence in all areas of the ice, not worrying too much about scoring, but only wanting to contain the Canadians in their own end, to break up plays between the blue lines, and to keep them to the outside in the attacking end.

Sidney Crosby had the best chance early on, but he couldn't turn and get a shot off with Grotnes down and out. Later in the period he was first to a loose puck in the slot and drilled a shot to the top corner that the goalie made a great save on. On a late power play he made the best pass of the period from his off wing, faking a shot and passing behind the play to Ryan Getzlaf. Getzlaf, however, fanned on the perfect set-up with an open net staring him straight in the eyes.

Sidney Crosby unleashes a slapshot while Norway's Patrick Thoresen looks on.

Second Period

Grotnes kept the team in the game until 2:30 of the second period. Canada, on the power play, struck on a nice little pass from Crosby to Jarome Iginla in the slot. Iginla's quick shot beat Grotnes to the stick side. Moments earlier, Shea Weber had hit the post with a slap shot of such ferocity replays showed the net rock back and forth.

The Canadians made it 2–0 at 4:27 when Dany Heatley made a nice touch off a Chris Pronger shot en route to the goal. The puck changed direction just enough to elude Grotnes under the blocker.

Canada's penalty killers were tested midway through the period when they had to kill a lengthy 5-on-3 situation, but they and Luongo passed with flying colours.

Mike Richards did what he does best several minutes later while killing a penalty. He shot the puck into the Norway end, but it bounced against the near side of the net. He banged away at it a couple of times, the second effort beating Grotnes between the pads. Eric Staal's penalty expired at the same time as the goal, 11:06, so technically it wasn't listed as a short-handed goal.

∧ *This over-sized flag made regular appearances at Canada Hockey Place during the Olympics.*

∨ *The netcam gives fans a view of what Norwegian goalie Pal Grotnes sees as Canada presses for a goal.*

Third Period

Canada found its rhythm and went into overdrive in the final 20 minutes. Getzlaf finally got a goal early in the period, moments after lifting a puck high over the empty net on a great chance. The goal came on a lengthy, delayed penalty and with a Norwegian defender without his stick. It was the last surrendered by Grotnes who was replaced by Andre Lysenstoen.

Dany Heatley gave the new goalie a rude awakening just a couple of minutes later on a power play. Skating down the left side, he wound up and let rip a fierce slap shot that beat Lysenstoen high on the short side.

Not to be outdone, Crosby, Nash, and Iginla scored just about the prettiest goal you'll ever see, Iginla finishing off a series of gorgeous passes that belied the newness of the threesome. Corey Perry and Iginla rounded out the scoring with late goals. The last set off a round of hat throwing from fans to honour Iginla's third goal of the game.

The blended officiating crew today featured NHLer Chris Rooney and Finn Jyri Ronn, both fluid skaters who read the flow of play well and who called the game judiciously. 🍁

^Grotnes makes a save as Canada's Corey Perry pressures him.

DAY 6

CANADA

CANADIAN OLYMPIC TEAM · ÉQUIPE OLYMPIQUE CANADIENNE

The Canada-Sweden game brought out fans of all sorts to cheer on their female heroes at UBC's Thunderbird Arena. As the Canadians romped to an easy 13–1 win, the audience had plenty of opportunity to cheer and shout their approval.

WOMEN'S HOCKEY

Displaying their trademark pit-bull aggression, Canada mauled Sweden 13–1 for a sold-out, jam-packed Thunderbird Arena at UBC's campus to clinch first place in Group A and set up a semifinals date with either Finland or the United States on February 22.

Meghan Agosta had three goals and two assists, and captain Hayley Wickenheiser had a goal and four assists.

It was one of the worst losses by the Swedes to Canada in international play, just marginally better than the 15–1 score in the first World Women's Championship in 1990 in Ottawa. The total number of goals for Canada in this preliminary round, 41, was also an Olympic record for a four-team, three-game group although still shy of the 50 scored by Canada in 1990.

"Our biggest focus coming in today was playing Sweden and not to look past them," said Gillian Apps. "I think things are really coming together with our team. We have a few days to prepare for the semis, and this is a really good environment to play in."

The game featured stretch passes and tic-tac-toe goals, a dominant and signature performance from Wickenheiser and Agosta, and an early warning call to the United States that the likely Gold-medal matchup will be one played at high speed and skill. All Sweden could do at the end of this game was sigh and head off the ice with overwhelmed admiration for Canada's superior play.

"I don't think this [result] is good or bad for the sport," said Becky Kellar. "I just felt they were really off today. The key to our success is that we've put a lot of effort into our national team."

First Period

The inevitability of Canada scoring the first goal was undeniable. From the drop of the puck through the first 6:58 when Meghan Agosta got her tournament-leading sixth goal, the pressure on Swedish goalie Kim Martin was as effective as it was relentless.

Canada finally scored on a gorgeous series of plays. First, Caroline Ouellette made a superb cross-ice, saucer pass from blue line to blue line to Cherie Piper, who took the puck along the right boards in full flight to create a two-on-one with Agosta. At that critical moment when Agosta arrived at the top of the crease with stick down, Piper drilled a hard and perfect pass that her teammate merely had to re-direct past Martin, who was playing the shooter, of course.

A little more than three minutes later, Canada struck again, on the power play, with another magnificent passing play. Hayley Wickenheiser made a perfect stretch pass to Agosta on the fly, and this time Agosta fed Marie-Philip Poulin who walked in and roofed a backhand over Martin's glove for a beautiful finish.

PRELIMINARY ROUND

CANADA 13

VS

SWEDEN 1

UBC THUNDERBIRD ARENA

WEDNESDAY, FEBRUARY 17, 2010

GAME SUMMARY

First Period

1. Canada, Agosta (Piper, Ouellette)	6:58
2. Canada, Poulin (Agosta, Wickenheiser)	9:16
3. Canada, Piper (Wickenheiser, Sostorics)	13:00
4. Canada, Vaillancourt (Johnston, Sostorics)	15:27
5. Canada, Bonhomme (Agosta)	15:57

Penalties: Andersson (SWE) 2:17, Eliasson (SWE) 7:52, Kingsbury (CAN) 17:50

Second Period

6. Canada, Agosta (Hefford)	1:06
7. Canada, Hefford (Ouellette, Kellar)	5:14
8. Canada, Wickenheiser (Apps)	5:36
9. Canada, Apps (Irwin, Piper)	6:13
10. Canada, Agosta (Ouellette)	7:59
11. Canada, Piper (Wickenheiser)	9:17
12. Canada, Irwin (Vaillancourt, Ward)	11:43

Penalties: Andersson (SWE) 7:26, Nevalainen (SWE) 9:59, Timglas (SWE—double minor) 13:15, Holst (SWE) 15:48

Third Period

13. Canada, Apps (MacLeod, Wickenheiser)	7:43
14. Sweden, Timglas (Jordansson, Rooth)	12:16

Penalties: Sostorics (CAN) 0:23, Kellar (CAN) 11:31, Poulin (CAN) 14:32, Rundqvist (SWE) 18:05

In Goal
Canada—St. Pierre 40 W 0 GA/Labonte 20 nd 1 GA
Sweden—Martin 28:47 L 10 GA/Grahn 31:13 nd 3 GA

Shots on Goal

Canada	23	20	9	52
Sweden	2	2	9	13

Referee—Wrazidlo (USA)
Linesmen—Majapuro (FIN) & Rolstad (USA)
Attendance: 5,483

Meghan Agosta led the tournament in scoring through the first three games with eight goals.

Sweden's goalie, Sarah Grahn faced an onslaught of Canadian offence after replacing starter Kim Martin, who surrendered ten goals.

The Swedes were reeling not only from the speed and skill of the pace, but high-energy play and creativity they simply couldn't match. At the 13-minute mark, the Canadians struck again, thanks to another long pass from Wickenheiser, this one to Piper. Going at top speed, she took the pass at the Swedes' blue line and walked in alone, her deke just squeezing through the pads of Martin.

The domination didn't end there. At 15:27 Rebecca Johnston walked in off the right boards and fed a great backhand pass across the crease to Sarah Vaillancourt who beat the beleaguered Martin with another perfect shot.

Thirty seconds later, the game was already out of reach when Tessa Bonhomme followed her shot to the crease. Martin couldn't control the rebound, and Bonhomme pushed it home for the ugliest goal of the period. The score was 5–0 after 20 of the most dominating minutes you'll ever see between these teams. Shots were an incredible 23–2.

Second Period

Nothing changed when teams came out for the second period. Just 66 seconds after the faceoff, all of which was played in the Swedish end, a mad scramble ensued and Agosta poked in a loose puck while all six Swedes tried to keep the puck out of the crease.

What could the Swedes do? Caroline Ouellette made a sensational back-pass to the short side behind the goal and Jayna Hefford ripped it to the top corner with target-practice skill to make it 7–0.

And then, everything Canada shot started to go in as if the entire team was Darryl Sittler playing in his ten-point game. Seconds later, they made it eight on a similar play except that Wickenheiser's shot hit a defenceman, bounced off Martin's glove, and dribbled into the net. Not as many marks for artistic impression as with Hefford's goal, but, as the expression goes, they all count.

The ninth goal came on another great pass, this from Haley Irwin to Gillian Apps. A distraught Martin remained in the net, but it was clear the Swedes had all but given up trying, a crucial mistake against a team they knew would never take the foot off the gas.

The tenth score came on a lucky bounce during a power play when Agosta's point shot hit a defender and beat Martin to the near side as she moved to the far side to make the save. The goal was her third of the game—her second hat trick in three games—and eighth of the Olympics. Less than a minute later, coach Peter Elander mercifully pulled Martin and inserted Sara Grahn in the net.

^Despite the presence of all six Swedes in the goal area, Canada scores again, this thanks to Meghan Agosta (#2), Jayna Hefford (#16), and Carla MacLeod (#5).

Gillian Apps helped Canada to a shockingly easy 13-1 route of the Swedes on this day.

(l to r) Cherie Piper, Hayley Wickenheiser, and Gillian Apps celebrate a goal during Canada's 13-1 landslide win versus Sweden.

Piper got her second when a Wickenheiser dash ended in a pass in front which went off Piper's skate and past Grahn. The 12th goal, on the power play, was another borne of sheer luck. Irwin barely got her stick on a pass in the slot, but it deflected off the stick off Emma Nordin into the top corner with crazy accuracy.

The only consolation in this disastrous period for Sweden was successfully killing off a four-minute minor penalty to Katarina Timglas which included 87 seconds of a 5-on-3 against the potent Canadian attack.

Third Period

The third period began with Charline Labonte in goal for Canada after Kim St. Pierre played the first 40 minutes and faced a grand total of four shots (to Canada's 43).

It took a while, but Canada added to the score line when Carla MacLeod's pass in front banked off of Apps's skate and in. Sweden's only goal came from Timglas on a goalmouth scramble during a power play.

"It was a pretty rough one out there today," said Sweden's captain, Erika Holst, "but we stepped it up in the third period. To keep up with Canada you have to play a close game and get some bounces, but that didn't happen. It felt like every puck went in for them."

Canada has a lengthy break until it plays again, but the team isn't worried. "I don't think we're going to be complacent," Kellar said. "The coaching staff has reminded us that we have five days off, but we'll be ready for the semis, for sure." ❦

More than 140 NHLers are here in Vancouver playing in what IIHF president Rene Fasel hopes will be the "pinnacle" of hockey. All is going so smoothly at this year's Olympics that the thing on almost everyone's mind is NHL participation in Sochi four years from now.

"Let me anticipate the one question I'm sure I'll be asked," NHL commissioner Gary Bettman said during his introductory remarks. Citing the many issues and challenges of going to the Olympics, he said there will not be a decision on NHL involvement in Sochi for quite a while. "Having said that, that doesn't mean we are going, and it doesn't mean we aren't. We have lots of time before we have to make a decision."

Fasel made no attempt to hide his desire for the continued presence of NHL players. "In four years, the NHL plays about 5,000 games. We believe it's worth it to play a few more at the Olympics. We very much want to see NHL players in 2014."

The difficulties and challenges of the NHL and IIHF merging the interests of the world's best league and the international game were most succinctly evident in one light exchange. In trying to explain the problems of Sochi, Fasel reflected and said: "The trouble is about two such different cultures. Gary is so American—and the Russians are so Russian." To which Bettman offered: "And, you, Rene, are so Switzerland."

Rene Fasel and Gary Bettman meet the press.

MEN'S HOCKEY

PRELIMINARY ROUND

CANADA  3

VS

SWITZERLAND 2

CANADA HOCKEY PLACE

THURSDAY, FEBRUARY 18, 2010

GAME SUMMARY

First Period
1. Canada, Heatley (Marleau, Toews)   9:21

Penalties: (SUI—too many men) 1:11, Seger (SUI)
6:43, Weber (CAN) 13:39

Second Period
2. Canada, Marleau (Heatley, Weber)   0:35
3. Switzerland, Ruthemann (Pluss, Paterlini) 8:59
4. Switzerland, von Gunten (Monnet, Furrer) 19:50

Penalties:

Third Period
No Scoring

Penalties: Paterlini (SUI) 17:09

Shootout
Goalies: Brodeur (CAN), Hiller (SUI)

SUI—Domenichelli—miss
CAN—Crosby—miss
SUI—Lemm—miss
CAN—Toews—miss
SUI—Wick—miss
CAN—Getzlaf—miss
CAN—Crosby—score
SUI—Pluss—miss

In Goal
Canada—Brodeur
Switzerland—Hiller

Shots on Goal

Canada	17	10	18	2	47
Switzerland	8	9	3	3	23

Referees—Larue (USA), Vinnerborg (SWE)
Linesmen—Feola (USA), Nowak (USA)

Attendance: 17,019

> *Martin Brodeur covers the lower half
> of the net against the Swiss.*

Sidney Crosby's shootout goal in the first round of sudden-death shootout gave Canada a dramatic and spectacular 3–2 victory at Canada Hockey Place. The win was sealed by Martin Brodeur's great glove save off Martin Pluss on the final shot.

This was the first non-playoff shootout in Olympic history.

Canada may have won the game, but the Swiss were also winners in a sense, having given Canada way more than it could handle for much of the game. Still, the home side avoided a second Olympic upset at the hands of Switzerland. It was, however, a far from easy victory and proved the 2–0 Swiss victory four years ago in Turin was no fluke.

Just as Canadian Paul DiPietro was in the lineup for the Swiss four years ago so too was Hnat Domenichelli (born in Edmonton, Alberta) in the lineup this year. But whereas DiPietro scored the only two goals in that victory—the first ever for Switzerland over Canada in Olympic history—Domenichelli was not a factor in this game, though several of his teammates were.

The win put Canada in second place in the Group A standings behind the United States, giving huge importance to their head-on meeting on February 21 for first place and a bye past the next round of qualification games.

"We had a decent start, but we got off our game plan in the second period," said Canadian defenceman Chris Pronger. "They play an NHL style and we knew it wasn't going to be easy."

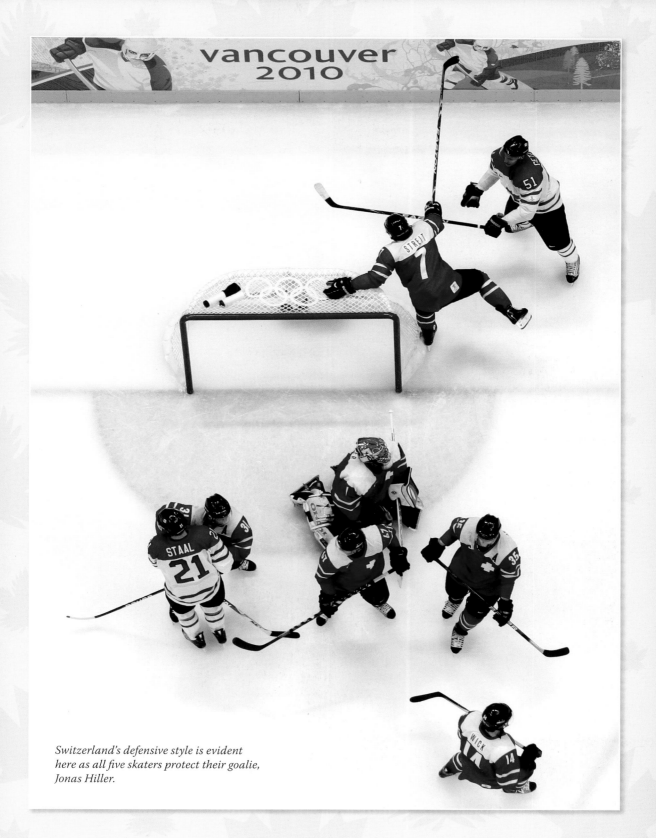

*Switzerland's defensive style is evident
here as all five skaters protect their goalie,
Jonas Hiller.*

^*Defenceman Dan Boyle carries the puck up ice.*

First Period

As with their first game against Norway, the Canadians struggled a bit in the early going. Switzerland had some decent scoring chances, and Canada failed to look impressive on two early power plays. The well-rested Brodeur, however, playing for Canada for the first time since Turin in 2006, turned aside every shot he faced with trademark poise and calm.

Dany Heatley got the first goal of the game at 9:21 as a result of a shoot-in. Canada roared in and claimed the loose puck, and Heatley swiped at it from the slot to the open side after Swiss goalie, Jonas Hiller, had committed to a pass going the other way. The goal quickly expunged the ghost of DiPietro from the Team Canada consciousness.

A couple of minutes later, Brodeur made a flashy glove save off a Rafael Diaz slapshot in the high slot, the best scoring chance of the period for La Suisse.

Second Period

It took only 35 seconds into the second period for Canada to make it 2–0 thanks to an early power play. Shea Weber's hard slapshot bounced off two players in front, and Patrick Marleau lifted the loose puck into the open side.

The teams opened up and went end to end for several minutes, exchanging scoring chances with entertaining regularity. Defenceman Dan Boyle slid across the crease to save a possible goal on one play, and Canada had several odd-man rushes it couldn't convert.

The Swiss got back in the game at 8:59 thanks to a poor decision by Drew Doughty to pinch at the Swiss blue line. He got caught out of position, and Ivo Ruthemann streaked down the left wing, ripping a shot past Brodeur's glove and off the far post and in. It was Doughty's last shift of the period as coach Mike Babcock sat the team's youngest player.

The Swiss dominated the rest of the period as Canada struggled with play in all areas of the ice. With each shift the Swiss grew more confident and the Canadians scrambled more and more. When the Swiss tied the game, it was a deserved reward for a period of strong play.

Chris Pronger took a selfish penalty by cross-checking an opponent along the boards, and Hiller raced to the bench for the extra attacker. Patrick von Gunten took a harmless shot toward the net from the left boards, and the puck caromed off the skate of Marleau and past a helpless Brodeur with just ten seconds left in the period. The stunned crowd watched as Canada skated off the ice in a 2–2 game, the Swiss feeling the score after two periods was a victory in and of itself.

"They got a lucky bounce off [Marleau's] skate, but they're a team that works hard and plays physically," Pronger noted.

Third Period

The reversal of fortunes continued in the third as the Swiss played with greater confidence and aggression. Canada played poorly in the defensive end and showed no effective creativity in the offensive end. Babcock shuffled his top line which had been Crosby-Nash-Iginla, replacing Iginla first with Patrice Bergeron and later Jonathan Toews.

Hiller did his part for the Swiss, making several spectacular saves, notably off a Getzlaf shot heading to the top corner and a one-timer by Heatley from in close. His performance was reminiscent of Martin Gerber's four years ago in that historic win, but he was bettered by Brodeur in the shootout.

Overtime

Both goalies stopped all three shots in the opening round, including Hiller on Crosby, but Babcock elected to go back to number 87 for the fourth Canadian shot and he didn't disappoint.

"It was a great effort from us," said Philippe Furrer. "We had great goaltending from Jonas who kept us in the game, and we had some scoring chances." ❧

Canada's Sidney Crosby protects the puck as he tries to go around defenceman Mark Streit of Switzerland.

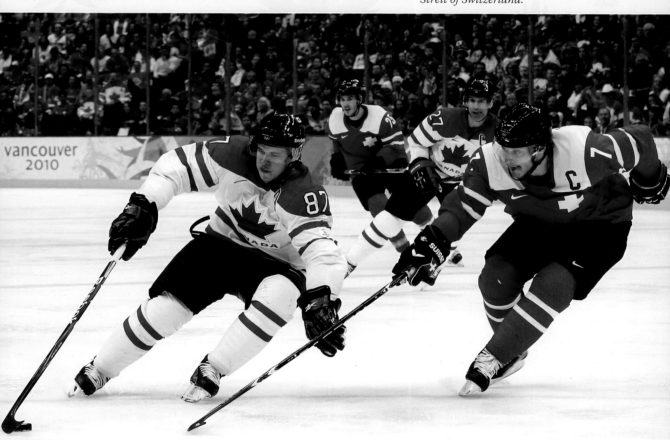

CANADA

CANADIAN OLYMPIC TEAM · ÉQUIPE OLYMPIQUE CANADIENNE

Friday, February 19, 2010

Wayne Gretzky paid a visit to Hockey House and offered his predictions to the hundreds of fans in attendance. He said Canada, Russia, Sweden, and the United States will be in the semifinals, and it will be the classic showdown for Gold— Canada and Russia. "And I pick Canada to win Gold," he said, as the cheers reached a deafening pitch.

Gretzky has been in town ever since the Opening Ceremony, when he lit the cauldron, and he made it clear that the team's narrow 3–2 shootout win over Switzerland is no reason to panic.

"The best thing that probably could have happened to this team was a close, tight game, and it shows this team can win under pressure," Gretzky said. "Going forward, I think they'll just get better and stronger every night."

^ *The cauldron is a unique, multi-flamed structure that sits in downtown Vancouver by the water.*

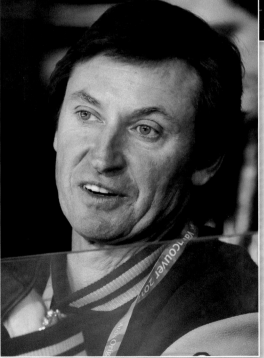

< *Wayne Gretzky has been around at several venues during the Olympics.*

As is always the case at international hockey tournaments, Canada is represented both by the players who wear the maple leaf but also by a clutch of players who play for another country. Vancouver 2010 is no exception. There were six Canadians by birth who appeared for other countries in the men's event, notably: Hnat Domenichelli (Switzerland); Jason Holland, T.J. Mulock, Chris Schmidt, and John Tripp (Germany); and Paul Stastny (United States).

Of these six, Domenichelli's is the most compelling story. Born in Alberta, he was selected 83rd overall by the Hartford Whalers in the 1994 Entry Draft while playing junior with the Kamloops Blazers. He won the Memorial Cup with the team in both 1995 and 1996, a rare accomplishment.

The seven years he spent in pro leagues in North America were peripatetic. Domenichelli made his NHL debut with the Whalers in 1996–97 and was soon traded to Calgary. He was later traded to Atlanta and Minnesota, but at each turn he spent more time in the minors than the NHL. Only in 2000–01 with the Thrashers did he play only in the NHL.

Domenichelli left for Switzerland in 2002, and has played in the top league there ever since. He married a Swiss woman, had two children with her, and in 2009, he finally obtained his Swiss passport, allowing him to play internationally for La Suisse.

His dramatic entry into the Olympic world came in the preliminary round game against Canada when the teams went to a shootout. Martin Brodeur stopped him, and Canada went on to win the game, 3–2.

Saturday, February 20, 2010

ⱽ*Hnat Domenichelli of Switzerland (right) was born in Canada but played in Vancouver for his new home.*

CANADA

CANADIAN OLYMPIC TEAM / ÉQUIPE OLYMPIQUE CANADIENNE

The final three preliminary round games played at Canada Hockey Place today were collectively billed as "Super Sunday"—and for good reason. By incredible coincidence, these games also represented the last three Gold-medal games at the NHL-attended Olympics. The first game was Russia-Czech Republic, the same teams which met for Gold in Nagano in 1998. The afternoon game was Canada-United States, the same as 2002 in Salt Lake. And, the late game featured Sweden and Finland, the finalists from Turin.

Without a doubt the Canada-United States game was the best, not only because of the crowd cheering on the home side, but because it was played at a higher tempo with greater physical presence than the other two. The disappointing loss, 5–3, represented a double whammy for Canada. First, by not winning a bye directly to the quarter-finals, it now had to play an extra game, against Germany in the qualifying round. Second, it meant that victory would set up a quarter-finals date with Russia, a dream matchup fans had craved, but one everyone wanted for Gold, not simply to advance to the semifinals.

American goalie Ryan Miller is down and out as six players surround him looking for the puck in the crease.

MEN'S HOCKEY

Hockey fans in Vancouver were treated to a new kind of hockey, played at a speed so fast only a small number of even the best players in the world can play. Canada-US's demonstration was, well, electrifying. Fans saw the lead change, great saves, end-to-end action, huge hits along the boards. This was Super Sunday hockey at its best and most heartbreaking. If this is only the preliminary round, it's unimaginable to think about the next round of games.

Defenceman Brian Rafalski had two first-period goals and added an assist in the win. Canada outshot the Americans, 45–23, but goalie Ryan Miller was excellent in the US net.

"Ryan Miller has been phenomenal," said US defenceman Jack Johnson, "and he bailed us out tonight when we were on our heels. It feels great. It's a huge win for us, but we didn't win any medals tonight. The wins coming up later this week are going to feel even better."

"I hate to say it, but maybe playing more games is what we need," Canadian goalie Martin Brodeur suggested. "We have things to work on in our game, and the next game will gives us that option."

First Period

The Americans stunned Canada by getting the puck deep off the opening faceoff and staying there until they got the first goal just 41 seconds later. They got a decent scoring chance after a few seconds, but Martin Brodeur made the save. Before the ensuing faceoff, coach Mike Babcock took Mike Richards off the Sidney Crosby line and put Patrice Bergeron back on the line for the rest of the shift.

Then, Brian Rafalski's routine point shot deflected in front off the unknowing stick of Crosby and past Brodeur to stun the pro-Canadian crowd and ignite American optimism.

GAME SUMMARY

First Period
1. United States, Rafalski (Suter, Langenbrunner) 0:41
2. Canada, Staal (Seabrook, Toews)   8:53
3. United States, Rafalski (unassisted)   9:15

Penalties: Getzlaf (CAN) 3:41, Pavelski (USA) 6:07

Second Period
4. Canada, Heatley (Toews, Weber)   3:32
5. United States, Drury (Ryan, Backes)   16:46

Penalties: Staal (CAN) 19:06

Third Period
6. United States, Langenbrunner (Rafalski, Suter) 7:09
7. Canada, Crosby (Nash, Keith)   16:51
8. United States, Kelser (Parise)   19:15 (en)

Penalties: Crosby (CAN) 1:44, Perry (CAN) 6:05, Kane (USA) 10:49, E. Johnson (USA) 14:56

In Goal
Canada—Brodeur
United States—Miller

Shots on Goal

Canada	19	12	14	45
United States	6	13	4	23

Referees—Watson (CAN) & Rooney (USA)
Linesmen—Sharrers (CAN) & Nelson (USA)

Attendance: 18,561

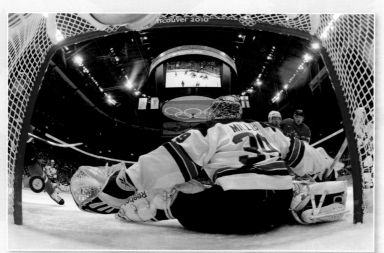

‹Ryan Miller was the difference in the game, making most of the tough saves while at the other end Martin Brodeur struggled.

Crosby then had a great shot on Ryan Miller, but the goalie made an excellent stop. Canada was getting under its collective legs, but the little momentum the players had was suspended by a goalie interference penalty to Ryan Getzlaf.

The Canadians killed this off then got a power play of their own, slowly working out the incredible nerves they had started the game with. They tied the game at 8:53 on a similar play to Rafalski's goal, except this time Eric Staal redirected Brent Seabrook's shot from the point.

Just 23 seconds later, Brodeur, who has played more games than any other goalie in NHL history, made a rookie-type error by batting at a puck from in front of his goal rather than controlling it or pushing it behind the net. Rafalski collected it inside the blue line, moved in, and beat Brodeur who gambled by sliding down to try to make the save. The puck still snuck under his pads and right into the net.

The crowd sagged noticeably, but the players got going and spent most of the rest of the period in the US end. Canada failed to tie the game before the end of the period, and the Americans looked plenty dangerous on the rare counter attacks they executed. In goal, Miller was rock solid. Shots on goal favoured Canada by a whopping 19–6 margin, but the Americans had the more important number—a 2–1 lead. This was unquestionably the fastest 20 minutes of hockey so far this year.

Jamie Langenbrunner tips a Brian Rafalski point shot past Brodeur for what turned out to be the winning goal, early in the third period.

^Big and mobile, Eric Staal comes out from
behind the net and tries to barge around
defenceman Ryan Suter.

Second Period

Canada picked up where it left off to start the second, dominating along the boards, controlling the puck, and maintaining possession in the American end. They tied the game at 3:32 on a wraparound attempt by Shea Weber. Miller got down to make the save, but Dany Heatley smacked in the rebound to the back side.

Now it was the Americans who were disorganized and on their heels. They had survived with the 2–1 lead long enough, and if they were to win, they'd have to press more and defend less.

Although Canada dominated the period, the US had several good scoring chances, and anyone who possibly doubted Brodeur's credentials in the first needn't have worried after three sensational pad saves to keep it a 2–2 game. At 16:44, though, the worrying resumed. Brodeur appeared to be knocked down in his crease, but then he lunged and missed a loose puck. Chris Drury snapped the puck into the wide open net to give the Americans a 3–2 lead despite being outplayed by a wide margin.

This goal set off the two most extraordinary minutes of hockey so far these Olympics. Both teams had two great chances on end-to-end rushes and breakaways, but both goalies were brilliant, and the teams headed to the dressing rooms after 40 minutes as they did after the first, with the Americans leading by a precious goal.

"We had a few lapses along the way. We bent, but we didn't break. Especially in the second period, we had a big goal late," said Ryan Malone.

Third Period

Buoyed by the end of the second, the Americans started the third as they did the first, and Canada stopped skating and checking. The result was penalty trouble, and the Americans capitalized at 7:09 on another deflected shot, this time by Jamie Langenbrunner.

Canada poured it on and made it 4–3 on a power play with just 3:09 to play, Crosby redirecting a pass from Rick Nash beautifully between Miller's pads. But Ryan Kesler got the empty netter by outskating a heavy-legged Corey Perry to a loose puck and sealing the victory.

"Miller made some great saves throughout the game," Crosby said. "He kept them in it. Throughout the third, we threw a lot at him, and he made some great saves. We took some penalties that took away from our momentum, but I thought each time we bounced back from those."

"I think you saw a lot of guys come together." Bobby Ryan noted. "Guys blocked some big shots, doing the dirty things for a win, and when you can say that about guys you've known for a week and played three games with, it's pretty remarkable." ❧

ᵛ *Sidney Crosby crashes the crease, but Ryan Miller keeps the puck out.*

CANADA

DAY 11

This was an historic day in hockey as the IIHF held a special ceremony to honour the inaugural 22 members of the Triple Gold Club. These players are the only ones to have won the Stanley Cup, Olympic Gold, and World Championship gold. Of the 22, there are nine Swedes, six Russians, five Canadians, and two Czechs.

The Canadians are Rob Blake, Joe Sakic, Brendan Shanahan, Chris Pronger, and Scott Niedermayer. Pronger and Niedermayer, of course, are on the current Team Canada roster.

The other members include Swedes Tomas Jonsson, Mats Naslund, Hakan Loob, Peter Forsberg, Nicklas Lidstrom, Fredrik Modin, Niklas Kronwall, Henrik Zetterberg, and Mikael Samuelsson.

The Russians are Valeri Kamensky, Alexei Gusarov, Slava Fetisov, Igor Larionov, Alexander Mogilny, and Vladimir Malakhov.

The two Czechs are Jaromir Jagr and Jiri Slegr.

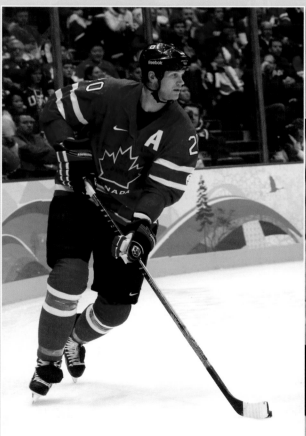

Chris Pronger (left) and Scott Niedermayer are two veteran defencemen on a Canadian team loaded with young stars.

43

WOMEN'S HOCKEY

SEMIFINAL

CANADA 5
VS
FINLAND 0

CANADA HOCKEY PLACE

MONDAY, FEBRUARY 22, 2010

GAME SUMMARY

First Period
1. Canada, Piper (Agosta, Hefford) 5:22
2. Canada, Irwin (unassisted) 14:36

Penalties: Hefford (CAN) 8:29, Voutilainen (FIN) 12:21, MacLeod (CAN) 18:33

Second Period
3. Canada, Agosta (Bonhomme, Hefford) 16:21

Penalties: Valimaki (FIN) 3:31, Kellar (CAN) 8:20, Lindstedt (FIN) 10:48, Voutilainen (V+FIN) 15:28, Apps (CAN) 15:45

Third Period
4. Canada, Irwin (Johnston, Vaillancourt) 4:23
5. Canada, Ouellette (Poulin) 18:57

Penalties: Tuominen (FIN) 0:47, Pelttari (FIN) 6:38, Vaillancourt (CAN) 17:50

In Goal
Canada—Szabados
Finland—Raty

Shots on Goal

Canada	15	17	18	50
Finland	2	3	6	11

Referee—Hertich (GER)
Linesmen—Skovbakke (DEN) & Rolstad (USA)

Attendance: 16,324

PAGE 45
Caroline Ouellette offers her arms for Marie-Philip Poulin after they combined for a late third-period goal.

Both Canada and Finland knew that a Gold-medal date with the United States was at stake in this game, the Americans having hammered Sweden, 9–1, in an earlier game at Canada Hockey Place. The three-day break, however, put a little rust in the Canadian attack as goals were hard to come by for the first time in the Olympics.

Shannon Szabados was the surprise starter for Canada, coach Melody Davidson showing great confidence in both her skaters and her backup goalie in such an important game.

First Period

Although Canada had the edge in play for the first few minutes, the Finns were hardly willing accomplices to another bad loss. They played smart defence in their own end and forechecked the Canadians at the other end, but Canada's superior skating and puck movement were also evident.

Canada drew first blood on a great play by Meghan Agosta. She chipped the puck in over the blue line and chased it down herself, skating in behind the goal and then feathering a beautiful back pass between two defenders to Cherie Piper. Her quick shot beat Noora Raty cleanly and gave Canada the early lead at 5:22.

After killing off a penalty, Canada nearly made it 2–0 but Gina Kingsbury hit the crossbar after a sensational solo effort by Jayna Hefford to get her the puck. A short time later, they scored on the power play at 14:36 when Tessa Bonhomme tried to jam the puck in on the short side as she went around the net. Raty made the save, but left the post exposed, allowing Haley Irwin to poke it in before she could be checked. Despite holding a 15–2 shots advantage, Canada ended the period leading by a 2–0 score.

Second Period

Although Canada dominated the second period by possession and territory, it faced its toughest period of hockey to date in Vancouver, thanks largely to the play of Finnish goalie, Raty. She didn't have to make too many spectacular saves, but she controlled almost every shot perfectly, giving up precious few rebounds and preventing Canada from getting those dangerous second and third shots.

It wasn't until 16:21 of the period that Canada scored, preventing a goalless period for what would have been the first time in Vancouver. Meghan Agosta, with her tournament-best ninth goal, made it 3–0 when she scooped up a loose puck just outside the crease and lifted it over a fallen Raty. The play began with a fine rush by Bonhomme who had gone to the net and disrupted Raty's concentration.

Moments later, Raty stopped Apps on a partial break with another great save, and the period ended with a surprisingly close 3–0 score, thanks largely to the goalie's fine play.

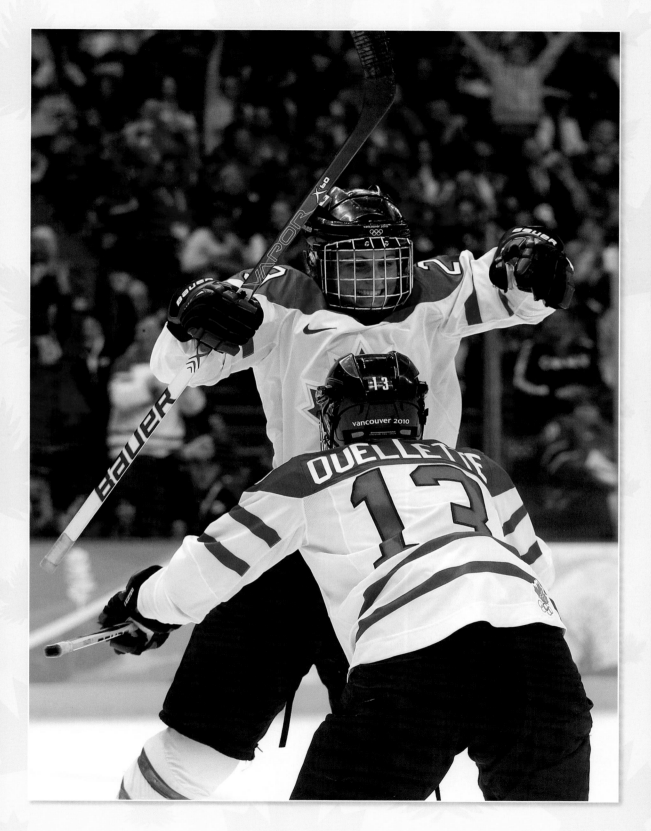

Canada's Meaghan Mikkelson stumbles in front of Finnish goalie Noora Raty while the puck goes into the net.

Jayna Hefford is stopped on this rush by Noora Raty, who had a spectacular game in limiting Canada to five goals.

Third Period

Canada came out flying in the final period and was rewarded early when Haley Irwin banged home a rebound in a scramble around Raty's goal. Canada kept pressing, and although it didn't get many great scoring chances, the defence also didn't give up many great chances, either.

Caroline Ouellette closed out the scoring with a late goal during a short-handed situation when she redirected a pass from the corner for the team's tournament-leading fourth short-handed goal.

The bottom line was that Canada and the United States were set for another Gold-medal showdown, the third of four Olympics in which this matchup has occurred. Every World Women's Championship since 1990 had also been a Canada-United States game. 🍁

CANADA

It was a difficult sight. There was Canada playing Germany in a must-win, elimination game—and at the end of the bench was goalie Martin Brodeur as Roberto Luongo took his place in the crease for the critical game.

Brodeur holds every major record for goalies—most games played, most wins, most shutouts. Internationally, he has represented Canada faithfully, successfully, and with pride and honour. He and partner Curtis Joseph helped Canada win silver at the 1996 World Championship, and then later that year Joseph was the number-one man at the World Cup while Brodeur patiently played two games as backup.

In 2002, Brodeur started as Joseph's backup again, this time at the Olympics, but after one game Brodeur took over and led Canada to an historic Gold medal. Brodeur won the World Cup in 2004 as the main man, and he led Canada to silver again at the 2005 World Championship. He was also the starter in 2006 and considered the main man for Vancouver here in 2010, but a sub-par performance during the team's 5–3 loss to the United States in the preliminary round forced coach Mike Babcock to make a change.

Has Brodeur played his last game in a Team Canada sweater? At age 37, he is toward the end of his career, and Babcock will likely have to go with Luongo the rest of the way in Vancouver. Just as Brodeur took over for Joseph eight years ago, Luongo has now taken over for Marty, one of the greatest goalies Team Canada has ever known.

Martin Brodeur (right) congratulates Roberto Luongo after Canada hammered Germany, 8-2 in the qualification round.

Team Canada eliminated Germany with an 8–2 win at Canada Hockey Place and, in doing so, may have found its first-line mojo just in time. The win advances the home side to the quarter-finals for a date with Russia in another win-or-go-home game.

Can you say Crosby vs. Ovechkin, Olympics edition? Believe it or not, the last time Canada beat the Russians (Soviets) in an Olympic hockey game was 50 years ago, in 1960 in Squaw Valley.

"Winning a game like this helps us out a lot," said 20-year-old defenceman Drew Doughty. "We were pretty down after losing that game to the US—a game I think we should have won, but being able to go out there like we did today and play well for 60 minutes will help us tomorrow."

Meanwhile, coach Mike Babcock got a great performance from the newly-formed threesome of centre Sidney Crosby, left winger Eric Staal, and right winger Jarome Iginla.

A loss to Germany might have been categorized as the worst in history for the country, given that this was an elimination game against a non-top-seven opponent.

First Period

Germany played their usual style of five men through the centre-ice area, content to try to bottle up the Canadians before they gained speed and could generate offence off the rush. Canada, meanwhile, came out strong for the first time at these Olympics, a promising sign even against such a defensive-minded opponent.

QUALIFICATION ROUND

CANADA		**8**
VS		
GERMANY		**2**

Canada Hockey Place

Tuesday, February 23, 2010

Game Summary

First Period
1. Canada, Thornton (Heatley, Keith)   10:13
Penalties: Schmidt (GER) 5:29

Second Period
2. Canada, Weber (Richards)   2:32
3. Canada, Iginla (Doughty, Staal)   3:41
4. Canada, Iginla (Staal, Boyle)   8:50
5. Germany, Goc (Schmidt, Muller)   16:34
Penalties: Seidenberg (GER) 3:26, Heatley (CAN) 4:15, Niedermayer (CAN) 6:34
Missed Penalty Shot: Crosby (CAN) 11:23

Third Period
6. Canada, Crosby (Staal, Keith)   1:10
7. Canada, Richards (Morrow, Toews)   6:41
8. Canada, Niedermayer (unassisted)   11:22
9. Canada, Nash (Pronger)   16:28
10. Germany, Klinge (Muller, Hospelt)   18:58
Penalties: Niedermayer (CAN) 9:03

In Goal
Canada—Luongo
Germany—Greiss

Shots on Goal

Canada	14	11	14	39
Germany	4	10	9	23

Referees—Ronn (FIN) & Rooney (USA)
Linesmen—Fonselius (FIN) & Murphy (USA)

Attendance: 17,723

< *Drew Doughty (left) celebrates a goal with Jarome Iginla.*

^ *Rick Nash goes one-on-one with Dennis Seidenberg.*

Canada finally got the first goal at 10:13, after holding a huge territorial and possession advantage through the first half of the period. Dany Heatley won a puck battle behind the net and got it out quickly to Joe Thornton at the back side of the net. Thornton snapped it home quickly, and while Canada had the 1–0 lead, the Germans were still looking for their first shot on goal.

That shot came at 11:44, and the final total for the period, 14–4, well reflected the margin of play in Canada's favour. Roberto Luongo—Bobby Lou to Vancouver Canucks fans—had just one difficult save to make after being named the starting goalie over Martin Brodeur, who had a rough outing two days ago against the United States.

Second Period

Play came to a halt at 3:10 for what turned out to be a critical decision. Shea Weber's point shot beat goalie Thomas Greiss and play carried on for half a minute until the next whistle. The referees communicated with the video-goal judge who reviewed the shot and discovered that the puck went through the net over Greiss's shoulder. A puck had gotten lodged in that very area during the warm-up and likely loosened the twine.

A minute later, Canada opened a 3–0 lead on the power play, Jarome Iginla stuffing in a rebound at 3:41 to give the team and fans some much needed breathing room.

That breathing room got a little tight when Canada took two penalties in quick succession, but the Canadians killed them off and scored soon after when Eric Staal came in with Crosby and Iginla on a three-on-two. Staal made a hard pass from the left wing to right, and as Greiss moved over, Iginla measured a wrist shot to the top corner, near side—a thing of beauty.

At 11:23 of the period, Rick Nash was awarded a penalty shot. He drove to the net and was pulled down, the play similar to how he scored the final goal of the 2007 World Championship in Moscow to cap a gold medal against Finland. International rules, however, allow any player to take the free shot. Babcock chose Crosby, but number 87 deked to the backhand and couldn't get the puck above Greiss's glove.

ᵛ*Eric Staal (#21) relishes one of Canada's eight goals.*

Marcel Goc got one back for the Germans at 16:34, when he collected an errant point shot behind the net and scored on a wraparound before Luongo could cover the back post. Crosby was caught on a long shift, using Toews's stick on the play after his broke earlier in the offensive end.

^Luongo and counterpart Thomas Greiss after the game.

Third Period

The new first line scored a highlight goal at 1:10 of the third. Duncan Keith drilled a hard pass from the left point to the right boards to Staal who, in turn, drilled a one-time pass to Crosby who had curled in front from behind the net to re-direct the puck past Greiss. That was the kind of creativity Canada had needed since its opening game against Norway.

Mike Richards made it 6–1 a short time later, and the result was now no longer in doubt. Niedermayer scored on a breakaway off a steal just inside his blue line. Nash closed the scoring for Canada with a great shot driving down his off wing.

Said Staal of the team's next opponent, "It's their offensive talent. Those two top lines are very high-powered. We're going to have to be good in our own end. Make sure we have good sticks. Hopefully we'll be on the attack to limit their chances. We'll have to be smart with the puck and make good decisions." 🍁

^Germany's Travis Mulock gets pinned along the boards by Mike Richards (left) as Jonathan Toews skates by.

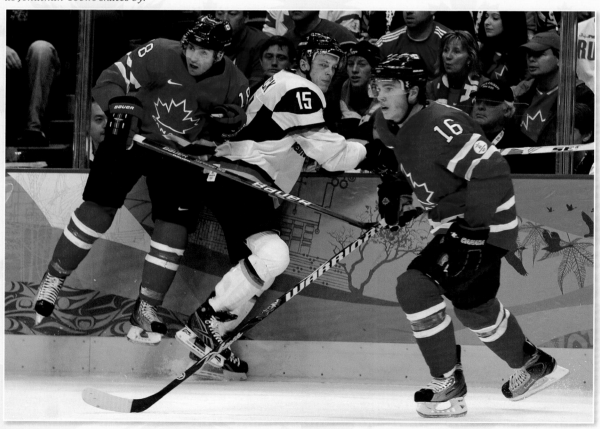

After the Soviet Union defeated Canada 2–0 in the 1956 Olympics, Canada got a measure of revenge four years later in Squaw Valley by walloping CCCP to the tune of 8–5—still the most goals the Soviets have ever allowed in a game.

Canada scored a 7–3 win over the Soviets in the final preliminary round game of the 1981 Canada Cup, but this score is significant for two reasons. First, coach Viktor Tikhonov employed his strategy to perfection when he started Vladimir Myshkin in goal ahead of Vladislav Tretiak. Wayne Gretzky had a goal and two assists, and Guy Lafleur had a goal and an assist to lead the attack.

The Soviets had already qualified for the playoff round, and Tikhonov didn't mind the lopsided loss because it softened Canada for the finals. Second, the softening worked to perfection, as Tretiak was brilliant in the finals and the Soviets waltzed to an 8–1 win.

We now have the score from February 24, 2010, a resounding 7–3 win by Canada, in the most recent chapter of the greatest and most intense international rivalry in the sport.

Shea Weber celebrates one of Canada's seven goals against the Russians.

MEN'S HOCKEY

QUARTERFINAL

CANADA **7**

VS

RUSSIA **3**

CANADA HOCKEY PLACE

WEDNESDAY, FEBRUARY 24, 2010

GAME SUMMARY

First Period
1. Canada, Getzlaf (Boyle, Pronger)   2:21
2. Canada, Boyle (Heatley, Marleau)   12:09
3. Canada, Nash (Toews, Richards)   12:55
4. Russia, Kalinin (Volchenkov, Fedorov)   14:39
5. Canada, Morrow (Boyle, Keith)   18:18

Penalties: Seabrook (CAN) 7:58, Volchenkov (RUS) 10:26

Second Period
6. Canada, Perry (Getzlaf, Keith)   3:10
7. Canada, Weber (Toews, Iginla)   4:07
8. Russia, Afinogenov (Kovalchuk, Grebeshkov)   4:46
9. Canada, Perry (Staal, Getzlaf)   9:51
10. Russia, Gonchar (Malkin)   11:40

Penalties: (CAN—too many men) 11:27, Korneyev (RUS) 12:58, Keith (CAN) 19:14

Third Period
No Scoring

Penalties: Gonchar (RUS) 2:01, (RUS—too many men) 5:11, Pronger (CAN) 14:37, Semin (RUS), Boyle (CAN) 17:17

In Goal
Canada—Luongo
Russia—Nabokov 24:07 L 6GA/Bryzgalov 35:53 nd 1 GA

Shots on Goal
Canada	21	9	12	42
Russia	12	8	8	28

Referees—Larue (USA) & Vinnerborg (SWE)
Linesmen—Nelson (USA) & Novak (SVK)

Attendance: 17,740

Canada beat Russia for the first time in the Olympics since 1960 (eight games), in a dominating fashion, winning 7–3 in a game that was lightning fast, although seldom close.

Corey Perry led the way with two goals and an assist. In all, six different players scored for Canada. Only in 1960, when Canada beat the Soviet Union by an 8–5 score in Squaw Valley, has the nation allowed more goals. It was also Canada's biggest win against Russia/Soviet Union in Olympic history.

Canada will now play in the semifinals on Friday at 6:30 pm local time against the winner of the Sweden-Slovakia game. For the Russians, the 2010 Olympic tournament is over.

"It was an electric atmosphere," said goalie Roberto Luongo, who is sure to start in the semifinal game. "It was really fun to play in. With the lead, it was a bit more comfortable."

Canada's strategy was simple: the game is being played on small ice, so play the small-ice game. This meant hitting Alexander Ovechkin every time he came near the puck, hitting anything and everything that moved, in fact. By the midway mark of the first period, no Russian player wanted to hang on to the puck for very long.

"It was a physical game on both sides of the puck," said Mike Richards. "Ovie is used to that from playing in the NHL. He's a marked guy every time he steps on the ice."

"They were much faster than us. They came out like gorillas out of a cage," said Russian goalkeeper Ilya Bryzgalov, who replaced Evgeni Nabokov after Canada's sixth goal.

First Period

The physical play had the Russians reeling, and the double whammy was the top-speed creativity the big-banging Canadians displayed once they had possession. Tic-tac-toe passes were the norm on every shift as Russian goalie Nabokov was sliding east and west trying to figure out who was shooting and who was passing.

Canada opened the scoring at 2:21. Defenceman Dan Boyle tore down the left wing and backhanded a pass to the slot where Getzlaf one-timed it past goalie Nabokov after defenceman Slava Kozlov failed to check Getzlaf with any purpose.

The Canadians kept pressing, moving the puck fluidly out of their own end and maintaining possession in the Russian end to create scoring chances. Nabokov looked nervous, and the Canadians played Ovechkin with the same physicality as 2004 when he was in the World Junior (U20) Championship gold-medal game.

Alexei Morozov had a good chance on a one-timer during a Russian power play, but he fanned on the shot. Ilya Kovalchuk let go another one-timer that made it through traffic, but Luongo came across to make a nice save as the penalty expired.

The frenetic pace continued. Crosby drove hard down the left side and was hauled down by Anton Volchenkov for a penalty. On the ensuing power play, a Boyle point shot was deftly redirected by Patrick Marleau through the pads of Nabokov for a 2–0 lead.

At 12:55, a fast break gave Canada a third goal, Nash finishing off a beautiful passing play up ice with Jonathan Toews and Mike Richards. Nash lifted the puck over Nabokov just as the goalie sprawled to try the Johnny Bower pokecheck. The astounding and relentless assault forced Russian coach Slava Bykov to call a timeout to try to settle down the team and quiet the crowd.

Indeed, the crowd grew silent, comfortable with the lead, and that's exactly how the Russians got one back at 14:39. Dmitri Kalinin's wrist shot from the point fooled Luongo and gave the Russians some life.

But Canada didn't surrender. The mostly Canadian-cheering crowd started up again, and the players continued to attack. The team got that crucial fourth goal late in the period. Brenden Morrow walked out from behind the goal and tried a backhand wraparound that rolled up Nabokov's body and behind him into the net for a 4–1 lead at 18:18. Shots favoured Canada 21–12 in quite possibly the fastest period of hockey ever played.

^ *Canada hasn't scored seven goals against the Russians since the 1981 Canada Cup.*

ᵛ *Corey Perry gets knocked down in front of Russian goalie Evgeni Nabokov by defenceman Fedor Tyutin.*

^Dan Boyle and Eric Staal are
stopped cold by Evgeni Nabokov.

Second Period

Canada made it a 5–1 game at 3:10 of the second off a harmless-looking play when Getzlaf skated in over the blue line surrounded by four Russians. He took a shot that was blocked, but Corey Perry banged home the loose puck past a surprised Nabokov. And still, Bykov left his goalie in the net.

Less than a minute later, Canada got another goal off a centre-ice turnover. Shea Weber finished things off with a bullet drive along the ice, off the far post and in at 4:07 to make it 6–1. This forced Nabokov to the showers in favour of Ilya Bryzgalov.

Just 39 seconds later, Ilya Kovalchuk found Maxim Afinogenov flying down the right wing. Afinogenov cut in around defenceman Duncan Keith and beat Luongo to the far side to cut the lead to four goals.

Just when it seemed the Canadians were sitting back and protecting the lead with half a game to play, they struck again on another gorgeous passing play. This time, Getzlaf carried the puck in over the Russian line and slipped a pass ahead to Staal who moved it across the ice to Perry. Perry's quick shot to the open side hit the net for his second of the night.

Luongo was then called upon to make his best save when Alexander Radulov was open in the slot. Radulov made a nice deke, but Luongo stuck out his left leg to make a great toe save.

A too-many-men penalty gave Russia a power play, and Sergei Gonchar beat Luongo with a long shot to cut the lead in this high-scoring game to 7–3. That's how the period ended to the delight of the crowd.

Third Period

Canada killed off an early penalty in the third and then lost Staal after he collided hard into the end boards chasing down a long pass. No penalty was called on the play, but on the ensuing rush Gonchar drew a hooking penalty. Iginla hit the post on one sequence but the score remained the same.

Luongo made his mark on the game by stoning Evgeni Malkin on a breakaway at 15:44, kicking out his right pad and sending the crowd into a frenetic "Loooo!"

"I thought our energy and execution right from the drop of the puck was phenomenal," Eric Staal noted. "We came out with jump. We were slowly boiling, and once the puck dropped to start the game, we were ready and firing. We got that goal to get us started right away, and the atmosphere and passion was unbelievable in here. It was a lot of fun out here."

Said a beleaguered Nabokov: "The first goal came too quick. They scored and just kept coming. We were not able to stop them, the shot differential [42–28] tells it all." ❧

∧*Surprisingly, neither Alexander Ovechkin nor Sidney Crosby played a significant role in the 7–3 score.*

∨*A close call for Roberto Luongo as a Russian shot zips by the far post.*

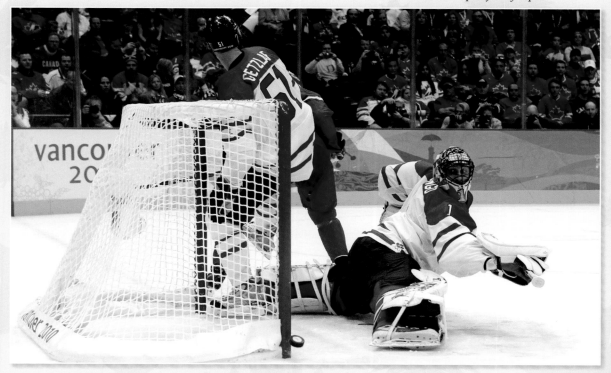

DAY 14

CANADA

Now that the Vancouver Olympics are down to four teams—Canada, Finland, Slovakia, and the United States—the other eight teams have gone their separate ways. Among those teams are several great players who may well have played their final game at the Olympics.

Consider Sweden's Nicklas Lidstrom, just shy of his 40th birthday, Daniel Alfredsson, 37 years old, and the oft-injured, 36-year-old Peter Forsberg. Their international careers have been long and full of success, but it's difficult to see either player in Sochi in 2014. Russia's

Sergei Fedorov, now 40 years old, surely won't be playing in four years. Thirty-eight-year-old Jaromir Jagr of the Czech Republic is also a sure Hall-of-Famer who won't be around.

These players have dedicated their lives to hockey and played the majority of their pro careers in the NHL. They are admired and respected in Canada as much as in Europe, and they are all top-drawer candidates for admission to the IIHF Hall of Fame in Zurich, Switzerland, and the Hockey Hall of Fame in Toronto.

ᵛ *More than any other Olympics, 2010 has been the last hurrah for many great players including Tre Kronor's Daniel Alfredsson.*

WOMEN'S HOCKEY

Marie-Philip Poulin scored two first-period goals to lead Canada to a third straight Olympic Gold medal in a 2–0 win over the United States. Shannon Szabados was nothing short of brilliant in goal for the Canadians, stopping all 28 shots.

"We trusted in ourselves," said veteran forward Jennifer Botterill. "Steve Yzerman came and spoke to us before the game, and that was one of his biggest pieces of advice: to trust yourself. We were excited, but had confidence in all the preparation we did."

Coming into this game, Szabados had only two games of top-level experience under her belt, both here in Vancouver over the last two weeks. The game was watched by Wayne Gretzky and Prime Minister Stephen Harper as well as a full complement of both men's teams from Canada and the US.

"I'm proud and very honoured to be Canadian," said Meghan Agosta, the MVP of these Olympics. "To represent your country in Canada is an honour in and of itself. We had no doubt that if we played hard and worked together that we would be successful."

First Period

Coach Melody Davidson gave Shannon Szabados the surprise start despite the many years of experience in Kim St. Pierre's resume. Six minutes into the game Szabados proved her worth—and Davidson's insightful choice—by making a huge glove save on Monique Lamoureux. Lamoureux flew down the left wing and ripped a wrist shot to the glove side, the game's first good scoring chance.

GOLD MEDAL GAME

CANADA **2**

VS

UNITED STATES 0

Canada Hockey Place

Thursday, February 25, 2010

GAME SUMMARY

First Period
1. Canada, Poulin (Botterill)   13:55
2. Canada, Poulin (Agosta)   16:50

Penalties: Potter (USA) 3:49, Chesson (USA) 8:18, Kingsbury (CAN) 10:00, Ward (CAN) 11:21, Hefford (CAN) 16:11, Zaugg-Siergiej (USA) 16:47

Second Period
No Scoring

Penalties: Hefford (CAN) 2:35, Kellar (CAN) 2:58, Cahow (USA) 10:01, Ruggiero (USA) 14:49, Hefford (CAN) 16:56

Third Period
No Scoring

Penalties: none

In Goal
Canada—Szabados
United States—Vetter

Shots on Goal

Canada	8	10	11	29
United States	7	14	7	28

Referee—Hove (NOR)
Linesmen—Richardson (CAN) & Rolstad (USA)

Attendance: 16,805

< *Three in a row! Players celebrate their incredible 2-0 victory over the United States in the Gold-medal game.*

Captain Hayley Wickenheiser jumps into the arms of goalie Shannon Szabados as the horn sounds to end the game.

While Canada's men had been scrutinized for the intense pressure they had felt, the women, with only easy games so far, hadn't faced any. But they started this game nervously and tentatively. Midway through the period, they skated their way into a more confident team, drawing a couple of penalties but unable to capitalize.

Then it was Canada that took two quick penalties, creating a five-on-three for the Americans for 38 seconds. Szabados was sensational, and Wickenheiser made an heroic sliding block of a hard shot to keep the US at bay. Soon after the teams were playing at full strength, Canada struck.

Jennifer Botterill took a loose puck along the left boards and swept a pass to Marie-Philip Poulin in the slot. Poulin ripped a one-timer over the glove of Jessie Vetter at 13:05.

Poulin got her second goal of the period at 16:50. This came off a faceoff deep in the US end to the left of Vetter. She won the draw to winger Meghan Agosta, but the weak backhander was easily blocked. The puck came right back to Poulin, however, and she drilled a low shot to the glove side which Vetter couldn't reach.

"Poulin's just a little sniper," said Botterill. "You try to get her the puck, and she gets off some good shots."

It was a fast and furious period marked by great scoring chances. The big difference was Szabados at one end and Canada's ability to nail its chances at the other.

PAGE 60

Haley Irwin collides mid-ice with Jocelyne Lamoureux, knocking the helmet off the American as she falls.

∧ Canada's Rebecca Johnston tries
to cut in on Jenny Potter.

PAGE 63 TOP
Goalie Shannon Szabados makes
one of her 28 saves during her
shutout performance.

PAGE 63 BOTTOM
Szabados's best save came via her
reflex flick of her glove to backhand
the puck over the top of the net.

Second Period

The Americans came out a determined group and spent most of the first 90 seconds of the second period in Canada's end, generating some good chances but unable to beat Szabados.

Canada then incurred two delay-of-game penalties within a span of 23 seconds, but the penalty killers during the 1:38 of US five-on-three were extraordinary. They blocked passing lanes, got sticks and bodies in the way of shots, and had Szabados as a superb last line of defence.

"Szabados played great," said Lamoureux. "She stole the game from us. We had two five-on-threes and we just couldn't bury the puck. They blocked a lot of shots. We had rebounds to capitalize on and she made some great saves. I tip my hat to her. She played awesome."

The rest of the period featured spectacularly exciting, end-to-end action. Both goalies had several close calls, the glove hand of Szabados often being the difference. Both teams also had their chances with the man advantage, and near the end of the period each team had a power play which was spent almost entirely in the offensive end. But after 40 heart-pounding minutes, Poulin's two goals were still the only ones on record.

Canada's outlet passing and poise under pressure were impressive, and the team was able to contain the speed on the

Americans for the most part, keeping their fleet-of-foot forwards to the outside. The Americans still generated their fair share of chances, and with a 2–0 score with 20 minutes (or more) to play, this game's result was by no means known.

Third Period

It was clear from the drop of the puck to start the third that Canada wasn't about to gamble, knowing that the Americans had to start taking chances. Szabados made another sensational save near the seven-minute mark. The Canadian defence made a dangerous clearing right through its own crease and the puck bounced off Monique Lamoureux's skate and headed right between the legs of the goalie until she squeezed her pads together.

The pace never let up, but the Canadians played brilliant defence and maintained their composure until the final horn when Canada Hockey Place erupted into a deafening cacophony of joy.

Canadian women had won hockey Gold for the third straight Olympics.

"This is definitely my last Olympic Games," Becky Kellar said, "and this is a good way to go out. It felt like a dream to be out there with that many people in the stands." ❧

ᵛ *The spontaneous team picture after victory, the players all smiles as they show their gold medals.*

Canada's women left nothing to chance. They wanted to stay sharp and focused every day they were in Vancouver, a tough task given that they had five days off between the preliminary round and the semifinals and another three days off between the semis and the Gold-medal game. So what did they do? They played hockey.

In fact, they played two exhibition games with the Vancouver North West Giants, one of the best midget teams in Canada. They played on February 12, the day before the Opening Ceremony, and again during their five-day layoff.

To keep their games secret, the team's itinerary listed these games under visits to the aquarium. No one in the media found out, and all players on the boys' team kept the games secret as well. "We had to stay sharp," said Melody Davidson, the team's coach. "We were winning 18–0, 13–1. We needed to stay sharp."

∨ *Goalie Shannon Szabados drapes herself in a Canadian flag with a gold maple leaf.*

MEN'S HOCKEY

CANADA 3

VS

SLOVAKIA 2

CANADA HOCKEY PLACE

FRIDAY, FEBRUARY 26, 2010

GAME SUMMARY

First Period
1. Canada, Marleau (Weber, Niedermayer)　13:30
2. Canada, Morrow (Pronger, Getzlaf)　15:17

Penalties: none

Second Period
3. Canada, Getzlaf (Perry, Pronger)　16:54

Penalties: Doughty (CAN) 1:29, Chara (SVK) 6:08, Zednik (SVK) 16:34

Third Period
4. Slovakia, Visnovsky (Stumpel)　11:35
5. Slovakia, Handzus (Zednik, Satan)　15:07

Penalties: none

In Goal
Canada—Luongo
Slovakia—Halak

Shots on Goal

Canada	10	11	7	28
Slovakia	4	5	12	21

Referees—LaRue (USA) & Ronn (FIN)
Linesmen—Fonselius (FIN) & Nelson (USA)

Attendance: 17,799

Just by the hair on their chinny-chin-chin did Canada survive the Slovakia scare tonight by a 3–2 score. Patrick Marleau, Brenden Morrow, and Ryan Getzlaf scored to send Canada on its way to victory in the semifinals at Canada Hockey Place.

Team Canada is now one Sunday-matinee win away from meeting the colossal expectations of the nation, but it will have to go through preliminary-round nemesis United States to win that cherished Gold medal.

The scenario is exactly the same as it was eight years ago in Salt Lake City when the two countries' women's team faced off for Gold as a preview to the men's final on February 24, 2002.

Slovakia, meanwhile, will face Finland for bronze on Saturday night.

"We still have a great chance tomorrow," Marian Hossa said. "We just have to regroup because today was a really tough game. It would be a dream come true if we got third place."

What seemed like a routine 3–0 lead after 40 minutes, turned tense when goalie Roberto Luongo looked weak on a couple of shots in the later stages of the third, making things more than a little uncomfortable for Canada.

Slovakia was a team unlike any other Canada had faced. It had the skill of the Czechs and the ability to play a tight, defensive game to perfection. As a result, play was tentative and choppy for several minutes and marked by several giveaways and bad decisions on both sides. By the midway point, though, Canada started to skate and find a little more room with and without the puck.

> *Goalie Roberto Luongo celebrates as time runs out on the Slovaks' comeback.*

First Period

The home side got the first goal at 13:30 on a nice series of passes inside the Slovakia end. Dany Heatley did the work along the boards and got the puck back to the point for Scott Niedermayer, who whipped a pass across to Weber at the other point. Weber snapped a quick shot a the goal, and Patrick Marleau deftly deflected the puck down between Halak's pads to give the Canadians the all-important first goal after video review confirmed it was not with a high stick that the puck was deflected.

Canada made it 2–0 less than two minutes later on a similar play. Ryan Getzlaf made a great play to get the puck back to Chris Pronger at the point, and Pronger got off a quick snap shot immediately which was again tipped in front, this time by Brenden Morrow.

Second Period

The second period repeated the first as Slovakia seemed content to play a very conservative game despite trailing by two, and Canada had difficulty generating speed out of its own end or creating scoring chances off the rush. It was close and hard hitting, but it was hardly the speedy poetry of the Canada-Russia game.

*^Jarome Iginla watches
Jaroslav Halak make a save.*

The only goal of the period came at 16:54 on a power play. A shot by Corey Perry was blocked in front and as Getzlaf was falling, he swiped a backhand over Halak to give the fans something to cheer about.

A minute later, Slovakia had its best chance to score off a bad giveaway in centre ice. Ziggy Palffy walked in alone, but as he was chased down, he let go a snap shot that Luongo closed the pads on.

Third Period

Slovakia got back in the game at 11:35 of the third when Lubomir Visnovsky banked a shot off Luongo on the near post from close to the red line.

"He was behind the net," said Luongo. ""t was a tough angle. It hit the post off my pad and went in. It is not something I wanted to happen but things do happen and you have to stay composed."

The Slovaks got their second at 15:07 when Michal Handzus batted a puck over Luongo after he failed to cover a shot on another wraparound, this from Richard Zednik. After that, mayhem ensued and the Slovaks nearly tied it in the final minute even with Halak on the bench.

*^Shea Weber knocks his man—and the
net—down in the Canadian end.*

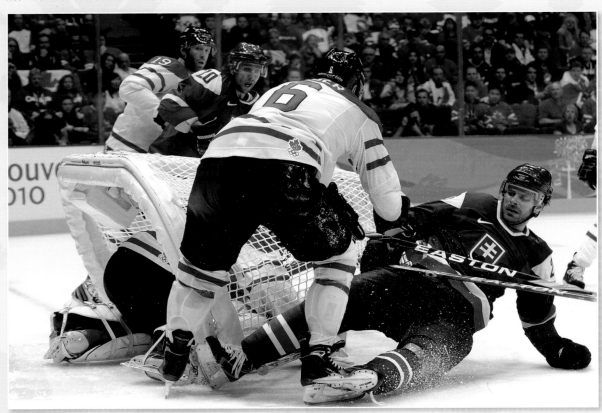

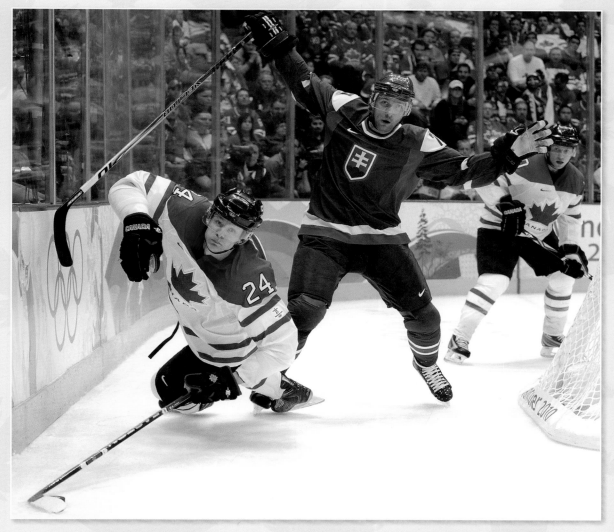

^ *Martin Strbak spreads his arms to show the referees he didn't knock down Corey Perry.*

"You have to give Canada credit," Hossa said. "This is one of the best teams I've ever played against. They are just great players. It's not easy to play against them."

Canada now advances to the Gold-medal game to face the Americans, a team it lost to, 5–3, during the preliminary round. This will be a fast, physical game that promises to be a classic.

"The Americans are going to come out hard," said CoreyPerry. "They're a hard, forechecking team, and they like to play kind of the same style we like to play. We'll have to be ready."

Pronger echoed these sentiments: "We've gotten to the Gold-medal game, but it's far from over. Obviously the US is playing well, with a lot of confidence. Their goalie is playing very well. We've got to play our best game of the tournament to win." ♣

CANADA

Mike Babcock, Canada's head coach, is on the verge of doing something no other coach has done: join the Triple Gold Club as a coach. No other bench boss in hockey history has won the Stanley Cup, World Championship gold, and Olympic Gold. Babcock won his Cup with Detroit in 2008 and led Canada to gold at the Worlds in 1997.

Of course, the reason this has never been done before is that European coaches have no chance of becoming head coaches in the NHL, let alone winning the Cup. And North American coaches likely get only one crack at coaching an Olympic team during their career. As a result, Babcock might well be the only Triple-Gold-Club coach for many years to come.

In addition to winning the Stanley Cup and World Championship, Babcock also coached Canada's Juniors to gold at the 1997 U20 championship.

DAY 17

Television audiences in 2010 have shattered all records. First, the finals of the World Junior Championship on TSN drew 12.3 million viewers for the Canada–United States gold-medal game on January 5, 2010.

The Canada–United States women's gold-medal game on February 25, 2010, had a peak audience of 11.3 million in Canada, a record for a women's hockey game.

But the Canada–United States men's preliminary round game was the most-watched show in Canadian television history. The average audience of 10.6 million translated into a monumental number—some 21.5 million Canadians (64 per cent of the population) tuned in to some part of the game.

The men's gold-medal game, another Canada–United States showdown, promises to shatter even these records. Stay tuned.

This moment is the most-watched in the history of television in Canada—Sidney Crosby's overtime goal for Olympic gold.

MEN'S HOCKEY

GOLD-MEDAL GAME

CANADA 3

VS

UNITED STATES 2

CANADA HOCKEY PLACE

SUNDAY, FEBRUARY 28, 2010

GAME SUMMARY

First Period
1. Canada, Toews (Richards)   12:50
Penalties: Ryan (USA) 14:02

Second Period
2. Canada, Perry (Getzlaf, Keith)   7:13
3. United States, Kesler (Kane)   12:44
Penalties: Malone (USA) 2:33, Staal (CAN) 4:41,
Toews (CAN) 8:25

Third Period
4. United States, Parise (Langenbrunner, Kane)   19:35
Penalties: none

Overtime
5. Canada, Crosby (Iginla)   7:40
Penalties: none

In Goal
Canada—Luongo
United States—Miller

Shots on Goal
Canada   10   15   7   7   39
United States   8   15   9   4   36

Referees—McCreary (CAN) & O'Halloran (CAN)
Linesmen—Fonselius (FIN) & Morin (CAN)
Attendance: 17,748

Sidney Crosby scored at 7:40 in overtime off a lovely pass from Jarome Iginla to give Canada gold on home ice. Crosby's quick, low shot beat Ryan Miller to give Canada a 3–2 win.

Likely the single-most anticipated game since hockey was brought indoors in 1875, this remarkable contest lived up to and exceeded its buildup.

"Every kid dreams of this opportunity [to score the game-winning goal in the Olympics]," said Crosby, "and any guy in that room could have done it. Doing it in Canada is the opportunity of a lifetime. You dream of that moment a thousand times growing up."

Crosby had been eerily quiet all game—the past three games, in fact—but as usual, he elevated his game to extraordinary heights at the exact moment required. In retrospect, who else could have scored the gold-medal-winning goal?

Jonathan Toews and Corey Perry scored for Canada and Ryan Kesler and Zach Parise for the United States in regulation before the teams came back out for 20 minutes of sudden death 4-on-4 hockey.

First Period
The game featured two teams with almost identical styles of play—both teams like to get the puck deep into enemy territory, chase it down, and cycle the puck to generate scoring chances—but on this day there was a twist.

As play began, it was clear that American coach Ron Wilson had told his players before the game to shoot the puck whenever, wherever the chance presented itself. In other words, make Canadian goalie Roberto Luongo handle the puck as much as possible.

As for the two NHL referees—Bill McCreary and Dan O'Halloran—they let the North Americans play a physical game, knowing that these quality players, appearing in the game of their lives, would not resort to cheap shots. "Let 'em play" was the order of the day, and with gold on the line, rightly so.

Canada opened the scoring at 12:50 on a harmless-looking play. The Americans won a faceoff deep in their own end and had the puck behind their net when Mike Richards checked Eric Johnson off the puck. Richards came out front with a shot that Ryan Miller saved, but the goalie didn't control the rebound.

Jonathan Toews snapped it home for the early and critical 1–0 lead. It was exactly the kind of play for which Richards was named to the team by executive director Steve Yzerman.

^Sidney Crosby gets tied up with
Ryan Callahan of the United States
but manages to move the puck up ice
all the same.

Second Period

The period was marked by good scoring chances at both ends, but also by many whistles and sometimes nervous play, and it ended with Canada in a slim lead.

Canada got an early power play in the second off a sloppy high sticking penalty by Ryan Malone at the Canadian blue line, but although there was good puck possession, there was no second goal. Moments later, Eric Staal was called for interference, and the Canadians had their first penalty-killing situation.

They passed with flying colours—and then got that vital second goal. Getzlaf came down the left side and tried to throw the puck in front, but the puck caromed off Ryan Whitney back to Corey Perry who had a whole open side as Miller was playing the initial pass. He made no mistake, and at 7:13 it was a 2–0 game.

The Americans got another power play moments later and came close with open play to the net, but Patrice Bergeron and Rick Nash led the penalty killers. After that, it was end-to-end action, heart-throbbing for fans of both teams.

^Canada and the U.S. played for the gold for the second time in the last three Olympics.

PAGE 75
Canada's Mike Richards collides with Ryan Suter along the boards.

PAGE 76°77
Sidney Crosby takes a pass from Jarome Iginla and snaps a low, quick shot to score the gold-medal goal for Canada. Teammates mob him in the corner.

And then it happened. At 12:44 the Americans got one back after a simple shot along the boards by Patrick Kane was redirected past Luongo, who got a piece of the shot, but not all of it. On the next shift, Zach Parise took a stretch pass down the left side and had another great chance. The Canadians' invincibility so far in the game was now in doubt, as was the outcome.

As in the first, there were great scoring chances, huge amounts of action around the crease of the two goalies, and no more goals. Canada was now 20 minutes from gold with a 2–1 lead, but it was a tenuous lead. The American speed to the outside was obvious, but Canada's strength up the middle was also very much in evidence. The best chance in the latter part of the period came when Staal took a long pass from Dan Boyle and shot over the net on a clear breakaway.

Third period

One shot, one bounce could ensure victory for Canada—or start an American comeback. That shot nearly came early in the third when a Chris Pronger point shot rattled off the post while Miller was screened. But the score remained the same.

Canada sat on the lead for the rest of the period, and it almost worked. But with Miller on the bench, Parise knocked in a loose puck from in front of Luongo's crease to force overtime.

"With 24 seconds left, we were obviously celebrating," Getzlaf admitted, "but our guys did a great job of believing and staying poised."

Said Staal: "We've got so many guys that have been through the Stanley Cups, Game Sevens, situations like that. We knew we just had to get back at it. There's nothing you can do. It's in the past. Obviously it was tough to give up that goal. At the end of the third, we just said: 'It's going to feel even better when we win it in overtime.' I'm sure it did for every Canadian out there."

Captain Scott Niedermayer agreed: "Lots of guys stepped up, and everybody kept their composure. We knew what we had to do: continue to go out and play our game, and just believe that it was going to happen."

Canada dominated the overtime, and when Crosby and Iginla came out they worked the puck along the left-wing boards. Crosby got the puck in the corner to Iginla and went to the net, shouting for the puck. "There was a certain urgency in his voice," Iginla said later, "so I just tried to get it to him before it was too late." Crosby's quick one-timer beat Miller cleanly, and an entire nation ran into the streets to celebrate the greatest goal since Paul Henderson's defining score in 1972.

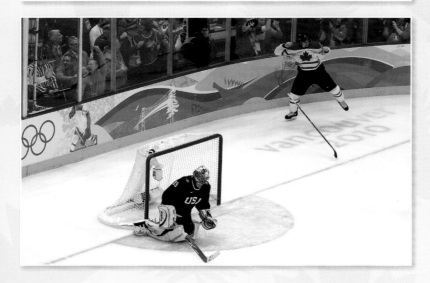

SLEDGE HOCKEY

CANADA

On January 4, 2010, Hockey Canada announced its sledge hockey team for the 2010 Vancouver Paralympics prior to the gold-medal game of the World Junior (U20) Championships in Saskatoon. Some 13 of the 15 players were returnees from the Gold-medal team in Turin four years previous.

2010 Sledge Hockey Team

Goal: Benoit St. Amand, Paul Rosen

Defence: Adam Dixon, Jean Labonte, Raymond Grassi, Graeme Murray

Forward: Herve Lord, Derek Whitson, Marc Dorion, Jeremy Booker, Shawn Matheson, Greg Westlake, Billy Bridges, Todd Nicholson, Bradley Bowden

The 2010 Paralympic Games run from March 13 to March 20 in Vancouver.

Group A—Czech Republic, Japan, South Korea, United States
Group B—Canada, Italy, Norway, Sweden

Canada's Preliminary Round Schedule
March 13 vs. Italy
March 14 vs. Sweden
March 16 vs. Norway

> *Bradley Bowden has been with Canada's sledge team since 1999.*

Results

Year	Event	Gold	Silver	Bronze	Host
1991	World Cup	CAN	SWE	NOR	Oslo, NOR
1992	World Cup	CAN	NOR	USA	Ottawa/Hull, CAN
1994	Paralympic Winter Games	SWE	NOR	CAN	Lillehammer, NOR
1996	World Championship	SWE	NOR	CAN	Nynahsam, SWE
1998	Paralympic Winter Games	NOR	CAN	SWE	Nagano, JPN
1999	Commemorative Games	CAN	NOR	SWE	Nagano, JPN
2000	World Championship	CAN	NOR	SWE	Salt Lake City, USA
2002	Paralympic Winter Games	USA	NOR	SWE	Salt Lake City, USA
2004	World Championship	NOR	USA	SWE	Ornskoldsvik, SWE
2006	Paralympic Winter Games	CAN	NOR	USA	Turin, ITA
2007	World Sledge Hockey Challenge	CAN	NOR	USA	Kelowna, CAN
2008	World Championship	CAN	NOR	USA	Marlborough, USA
2009	World Sledge Hockey Challenge	USA	CAN	NOR	Charlottetown, CAN

^ *Jean Labonte in action against the United States.*

The Origins

Sledge hockey was created in the early 1960s by two Swedes at a rehabilitation centre in Stockholm. It wasn't until 1969 that games between European nations took place. In 1981, Great Britain started a team and the next year Canada joined. The United States entered the competition in 1990, and three years later, Estonia and Japan joined. 1994 was a breakthrough year for the sport as it became part of the Paralympic Games, the quadrennial event which followed the Olympic Winter Games. In 2004, sledge hockey became a fully recognized sport by Hockey Canada.

The Rules

First drawn up in 1990 and based on Canadian hockey rules, sledge hockey rules are virtually identical save for a few which specifically address players' needs. The sledge must consist of a metal frame with two blades under which the puck can pass. Entranceways to benches are at ice level so players can slide on and off the ice easily. Sticks are curved at one end and have small picks at the other so that players can push themselves around the ice using the butt-end of the shaft. To this end, each player is allowed two sticks, one for each hand. Helmets are mandatory. Games consist of a standard three periods of 20 minutes each, and teams play five skaters a side (plus a goalie).

˅ *Fifty-one-year-old Herve Lord goes back to 1991 with the sledge hockey program.*

^Shawn Matheson started with the team in 1989 as a 17-year-old.

^Matheson fights for a loose puck with two American players.

>Matheson is the great-great-grandson of John Mercer Johnson, one of the Fathers of Confederation.

BERGERON, PATRICE

ANCIENNE-LORETTE, QUEBEC, JULY 24, 1985

CENTRE

SHOOTS RIGHT

6'2" 194 LBS

NHL TEAM: BOSTON BRUINS

Patrice Bergeron's rise to the top of the NHL was meteoric, to say the least. Drafted 45th overall by Boston in 2003, he joined the Bruins that fall at 18, and had a fine rookie season, scoring 39 points and earning a +5 rating on a weak defensive team. The Bruins lost in the first round of the playoffs, and Bergeron accepted an invitation to play for Canada at the World Championship. Three weeks later, he had a gold medal around his neck.

The next season was wiped out because of the lockout, so Bergeron played for Boston's AHL affiliate in Providence. Over Christmas, however, he was loaned to the Canadian junior team and, paired with 18-year-old Sidney Crosby, helped Canada win gold. Bergeron led the tournament in points and was named MVP, setting a record that may never be beaten by becoming the first player in IIHF history to win gold at the senior men's World Championship before winning World Junior Championship gold.

He was back to the NHL for 2005–06, and had a spectacular season, giving the Bruins hope that they had drafted a true superstar in the making. Bergeron had 31 goals and 73 points, but the Bruins missed the playoffs. Bergeron went back to the World Championship and teamed with Crosby again, but this time it was Crosby who led the tournament in scoring although Canada finished a disappointing fourth.

After another fine season, Bergeron's world came undone in just the tenth game of the 2007–08 season. He was hammered from behind into the boards by Randy Jones, lost consciousness, and was carried off the ice on a stretcher. He tried to return on a couple of occasions, but the post-concussion syndrome was so severe he missed the rest of the season and couldn't properly train again until the following summer.

Bergeron has slowly but surely returned to top form, and part of his being named to the 2010 Olympic team must have been his previous tournament play with Crosby. A scorer with good vision of the ice for passing, Bergeron is a world-class player in any game he competes in.

INTERNATIONAL STATISTICS			GP	G	A	P	Pim	Place
2004 WM	CAN		9	1	0	1	4	G
2005 U20	CAN		6	5	8	13	6	G
2006 WM	CAN		9	6	8	14	2	4th

BOYLE, DAN

OTTAWA, ONTARIO,
JULY 12, 1976

DEFENCE

SHOOTS RIGHT

5'11" 190 LBS

NHL TEAM: SAN JOSE SHARKS

CANADA

That Dan Boyle is playing in the NHL, let alone the Olympics, is a testament to his character and ambition, his desire to let no man or word stand in between he and success. He was, after all, completely ignored at the NHL draft during his years of eligibility, playing four full years at Miami University (in Ohio) before being signed as a free agent by the Florida Panthers.

But just because the Panthers signed him did not mean he was on Easy Street. Indeed, he played his first three years more with the farm team than in the NHL, and early in his fourth season the Panthers decided he wasn't going to be a contributor, trading him to Tampa Bay for nothing more than a 5th-round draft choice.

When he got to Tampa Bay, however, he was joining a team on the cusp of greatness. Despite the immense talent of players around him, he was getting more ice time than he ever had at this level. The core of the Lightning included the trio of great forwards—Vincent Lecavalier, Martin St. Louis, and Brad Richards—and Boyle fit right in with his skating, passing, and offensive abilities from the blue line.

In just his second full season with the team, the Lightning won the Stanley Cup, and the image of Boyle drinking champagne from the sacred silverware in 2004 was one he never could have conjured during his days playing in Ohio with a team nicknamed the Redhawks.

This win came just before the NHL's darkest hour when a full season was lost because of the lockout, but Boyle would have nothing to do with being idle for a year. He went to Sweden and played with Djurgarden, and was then invited to play for Canada for the first time, at the World Championship. He helped the team win silver, and the following year was back with the Lightning.

Boyle was asked to be a member of Canada's "taxi squad" for the 2006 Olympics in Turin, one of three players (with Eric Staal and Jason Spezza) who would come to Turin, practice on their own, and play only in case of injury. He didn't complain, made the journey, and gained what experience he could. He then returned home to re-join the Lightning.

The team, though, had serious problems on and off the ice, and it was a blessing that he was traded to San Jose in the summer of 2008. The Sharks were another team with immense talent, but had been frustratingly unsuccessful in the playoffs. Still, Boyle fit in on a team similar to what he joined in Tampa Bay, surrounded by talent such as Joe Thornton and Patrick Marleau, teammates in Vancouver.

INTERNATIONAL STATISTICS			GP	G	A	P	Pim	Place
2005	WM	CAN	9	0	3	3	6	S

BRODEUR, MARTIN

MONTREAL, QUEBEC,
MAY 6, 1972

GOALIE

CATCHES RIGHT

6'1" 205 LBS

NHL TEAM: NEW JERSEY DEVILS

CANADA

Martin Brodeur now holds pretty much every NHL record for goalies that's worth holding. During the current season he eclipsed Terry Sawchuk's regular-season record of 103 shutouts, and he also holds the record for combined regular season and playoff shutouts. He has won more games than any other goalie, played in more games, and appeared for more minutes than anyone else. He is the only goalie to win at least 30 games for an incredible 12 seasons in a row, and he has seven seasons of 40 wins or more—also a record.

Drafted 20th overall by New Jersey in 1990, Brodeur kept playing junior in Quebec for most of the next three seasons. In 1993–94, he became the team's number-one goalie, posting a 27–11–8 record and winning the Calder Trophy. For the last 16 seasons he has remained the number-one man, earning many other individual awards along the way. The only blip on his otherwise impeccable record came last year when he missed many weeks with an elbow injury that required surgery, but he bounced back to lead the Devils to the playoffs again. In fact, the Devils have made the playoffs every year but one with Brodeur in the net.

Brodeur has taken the Devils to three Stanley Cup wins—the only three in franchise history. The first came unexpectedly, at the end of the shortened season of 1994–95, but the second, in 2000, came as a surprise to no one. The most recent win came in 2003, and during that playoff run Brodeur earned a playoff record seven shutouts.

In addition, Brodeur has won the Vezina Trophy four times and the Jennings Trophy four times. Apart from his ability to stop the puck, he is known as one of the greatest puck-handling goalies of all time as well. He has scored two goals, one in the regular season and another in the playoffs.

If his NHL resume is impeccable, his international accomplishments aren't far behind. Of course, nothing ranks higher than the Gold medal he won with Team Canada at the 2002 Olympics. He later led Canada to victory at the 2004 World Cup, and twice he has come within a win to become the only goalie to join the Triple Gold Club for winning the Stanley Cup, Olympic Gold and the World Championship. Brodeur won silver at the Worlds in both 1996 and 2005. Brodeur and his father, Denis, are the only father-son pair in Canadian history to have both won Olympic medals in hockey. Denis won bronze at the 1956 Olympics.

INTERNATIONAL STATISTICS						Mins	GA	SO	GAA	A	Pim	Place
				GP	W-T-L							
1996	WM	CAN		3	0-1-1	140:00	8	0	3.43	0	0	S
1996	WCH	CAN		2	0-0-1	60:02	4	0	4.00	0	0	2nd
2002	OG	CAN		5	4-1-0	300:00	9	0	1.80	0	0	G
2004	WCH	CAN		5	5-0-0	300:00	5	1	1.00	0	2	1st
2005	WM	CAN		7	5-0-2	418:36	20	0	2.87	0	0	S
2006	OG	CAN		4	2-0-2	238:40	8	0	2.01	0	0	7th

CROSBY, SIDNEY

COLE HARBOUR, NOVA SCOTIA,
AUGUST 7, 1987

CENTRE

SHOOTS LEFT

5'11" 200 LBS

NHL TEAM: PITTSBURGH PENGUINS

Even if Sidney Crosby never plays another game, he will still be considered one of the greats. Such has been the immediate and explosive impact he has had on the game. Crosby was the 1st overall selection in the 2005 Entry Draft, a draft that's order was chosen by lottery after the lockout wiped out the previous season. Incredibly, Mario Lemieux and the Penguins got the coveted first choice, and the Hall-of-Fame veteran (and team owner) worked with the teenager to resuscitate hockey in Pittsburgh.

Crosby had 102 points as a rookie, breaking Lemieux's team record, but more importantly he was the face of the "new" NHL after the lockout. He had powerful strides and breakaway speed. He was great in the corner and equally great one-on-one, a superb passer and dangerous shooter.

In junior, with Rimouski, Crosby was unstoppable. He led the QMJHL in scoring at age 17 and again at 18, taking the team to the Memorial Cup in 2005 where he led the tournament in scoring and was named MVP. He played at two World Junior Championships as well, losing to Russia in the 2004 finals and vowing revenge the next year. True to his word, he led Canada to gold in 2005, its first of five in a row.

Despite his fine rookie showing with the Penguins in 2005–06, the team missed the playoffs and Crosby went to play for Canada at the World Championship. He dominated, leading the tournament in scoring and becoming the youngest player in IIHF history to do so.

But Crosby was only just beginning. The next NHL season he led the league in scoring to win the Art Ross Trophy but also won the Hart Trophy and Lester B. Pearson Award. The team lost in the first round of the playoffs, but Crosby, as always, learned from the defeat. In 2007–08, he suffered a sprain high in his ankle and missed several weeks. While the injury prevented him from reaching 100 points in the season, it left him fresh for the playoffs. Crosby led the Pens to the Cup finals for the first time since 1992 when Lemieux had done same, but the team lost to Detroit in six games.

Everything fell into place in 2008–09. Crosby again reached the 100-point mark in the regular season, and yet again in the playoffs he took the Pens to the finals for a rematch with Detroit. Along the way, he played his best hockey in an early playoff date with Washington, facing arch-rival Alexander Ovechkin in one of the most exciting playoff series of the modern era. Both players were extraordinary, but Crosby prevailed. The Pens went on to beat Detroit at the Joe Louis Arena in game seven. Crosby became the youngest Cup-winning captain in Stanley Cup history.

INTERNATIONAL STATISTICS							
			GP	G	A	P	Pim	Place
2004 U20	CAN	6	2	3	5	4	S
2005 U20	CAN	6	6	3	9	4	G
2006 WM	CAN	9	8	8	16	10	4th

DOUGHTY, DREW

LONDON, ONTARIO, DECEMBER 8, 1989

DEFENCE

SHOOTS RIGHT

6'1" 203 LBS

NHL TEAM: LOS ANGELES KINGS

One of the "would he or wouldn't he" players people talked about at the start of the 2009–10 season, Drew Doughty would, indeed, be one of the 23 players named to Team Canada by executive director Steve Yzerman, even though Doughty had just turned 20 years old before the announcement. He is the team's youngest player.

But there was wisdom and careful thought behind Yzerman's selection, not the least of which was that players, coaches, and managers around the league all concurred that the youngster played with a maturity and poise far beyond his years.

He played junior with the Guelph Storm of the OHL, and midway through the 2007–08 season was invited to play for Canada.at the World Junior Championship. Not only did he help the country win gold, he was named best defenceman by the tournament directorate.

Drafted 2nd overall by Los Angeles in 2008, Doughty jumped into the lineup right away and was one of the youngest players in the NHL during the 2008–09 season. No matter. He averaged nearly 24 minutes of playing time a game, appeared in 81 of the team's 82 games, and was the team's best defenceman despite being only 18 years old. He was on a rebuilding Kings team, and when they failed to make the playoffs, he was invited to play for Canada at the World Championship. Despite the increase in quality of hockey, Doughty was again a star and helped Canada win a silver medal after falling 2–1 to Russia in the gold-medal game.

What has separated him from other young players is his ability to stay calm under pressure, to make a smart decision instead of panicking and giving the puck away. He plays with confidence and moves play up ice effectively, showing evermore offensive ability as his confidence increases. He is, in short, the kind of defenceman who will be asked to represent Canada for a long time.

INTERNATIONAL STATISTICS			GP	G	A	P	Pim	Place
2007	U18	CAN	6	2	3	5	8	4th
2008	U20	CAN	7	0	4	4	0	G
2009	WM	CAN	9	1	6	7	4	S

FLEURY, MARC-ANDRE

SOREL, QUEBEC,
NOVEMBER 28, 1984

GOALIE

CATCHES LEFT

6'2" 180 LBS

NHL TEAM: PITTSBURGH PENGUINS

One of only three goalies to be drafted first overall—after Michel Plasse and Rick DiPietro—Marc-Andre Fleury took a while to develop into the Stanley Cup winner he became in June of 2009. He was drafted by Pittsburgh in 2003 toward the end of a superb junior career with the Cape Breton Screaming Eagles, who later retired his number 29.

Fleury began the 2003–04 season with the Penguins and made 46 saves in his debut on October 10 versus the Los Angeles Kings. Things went downhill form there, though, as the team struggled defensively. It was not a good place for a rookie goalie to be, so the Penguins loaned him to Team Canada for the World Junior Championship and then sent him back to Cape Breton. He later appeared for the farm team in Wilkes-Barre for the playoffs. The next year was a lost season for the NHL because of the lockout, but this might have been a blessing in disguise for Fleury. He spent the full season in the AHL and gained confidence, without feeling the pressure of needing to make it to the NHL right away.

By the start of 2005–06, not only was he a more experienced goalie, the team now had Sidney Crosby in the lineup to orchestrate the offense. Fleury competed for playing time with Sebastien Caron and Jocelyn Thibault, but by season's end, he was the number-one man, even though the team still struggled to win games. The year after, he was sensational, posting a record of 40–16–9 and helping the Pens to the playoffs. Although they lost in the first round to Ottawa in five games, things were looking up for the team.

The next season started well for the goalie but he suffered an ankle sprain that kept him out of the lineup for nearly two months. He didn't return until late in the season, but the extra rest did him good in the playoffs as the Penguins marched all the way to the Cup finals. They lost to Detroit in six games, but it was clear this was a team that would win the Stanley Cup sooner rather than later.

Sooner, in fact, came the next year. After a coaching change mid-season, Fleury and the Penguins went back to the finals against Detroit, but this time Pittsburgh prevailed, winning game seven in Detroit 2–1. The victory was sealed when Fleury made a diving save off a Nicklas Lidstrom shot in the dying seconds.

INTERNATIONAL STATISTICS										
		GP	W-T-L	Mins	GA	SO	GAA	A	Pim	Place
2003 U20	CAN	5	4-0-1	267:28	7	1	1.57	1	0	S
2004 U20	CAN	5	4-0-1	298:51	9	1	1.81	0	2	S

Fleury, Marc-Andre   97

GETZLAF, RYAN

REGINA, SASKATCHEWAN,
MAY 10, 1985

CENTRE

SHOOTS RIGHT

6'4" 221 LBS

NHL TEAM: ANAHEIM DUCKS

One of many talented young guns on Canada's 2010 team, Ryan Getzlaf has a combination of attributes that led to his inclusion. First, he has international experience. Second, he has developed into one of the most complete, young players in the game. Third, he's a winner.

Getzlaf was in the middle of his junior career with the Calgary Hitmen when he was drafted 19th overall by Anaheim in 2003. At the end of his fourth year, he left junior and joined the Duck's farm team in Cincinnati during their Calder Cup playoffs, appearing in his first ten pro games. The next fall, he made the Ducks and began his NHL career.

His junior career was punctuated by success at the international level. Getzlaf won gold at the World U18 Championship, and then, playing with Sidney Crosby, won a silver and gold medal in consecutive World Junior Championships, in 2004 and 2005.

Big and rangy, Getzlaf took a bit of time to develop, although from day one he showed the skill and determination that proved he would one day be a star. He scored 14 goals as a rookie, and then in each of his next three seasons scored 25, 24, and 25 goals, a virtual model of consistency. In each year, though, his assists totals increased thanks to greater experience as well as playing on a line with Dustin Penner and Corey Perry. Dubbed the Kid Line, this threesome became the team's number-one line.

In just his second season, Getzlaf helped the Ducks win the Stanley Cup. He led the team in playoff scoring, and they beat Ottawa in five games to bring the Stanley Cup to California for the first time in hockey history. Early the next season, the Ducks signed him to a five-year, $26.6-million contract extension, and a short time later signed Perry to the same deal.

Anaheim was eliminated in the opening round of the playoffs at the end of that year, so Getzlaf joined Team Canada for the World Championship in Quebec City, the first time the nation had ever hosted the event. Getzlaf was dominant, leading the team to the gold-medal game where it lost to Russia, 5–4, in overtime.

INTERNATIONAL STATISTICS							
		GP	G	A	P	Pim	Place
2003 U18	CAN	7	2	2	4	10	G
2004 U20	CAN	6	3	3	6	4	S
2005 U20	CAN	6	3	9	12	8	G
2008 WM	CAN	9	3	11	14	10	S

HEATLEY, DANY

FREIBURG, WEST GERMANY (GERMANY), JANUARY 21, 1981

LEFT WING

SHOOTS LEFT

6'4" 221 LBS

NHL TEAM: SAN JOSE SHARKS

One of the most prolific scorers since the NHL returned after the lockout in 2005, and one of the most frequent representatives of Team Canada of all time, Dany Heatley has both a deadly shot and a maple leaf tattooed on his heart. Although he has not been blessed with great success in the Stanley Cup playoffs, he has been victorious at virtually every level of international play during his decade of hockey.

He was drafted 2nd overall by Atlanta in 2000 (behind only Rick DiPietro). Heatley played just one more year of NCAA at the University of Wisconsin before embarking on an NHL career. As a rookie, he scored 26 goals and won the Calder Trophy, displaying quick hands and a deadly shot from all areas inside the blue line. A year later, he increased his goal total to 41.

Heatley's career in Atlanta ended after an horrific car accident, and, seeking a fresh start, he was traded to Ottawa after the lockout where he developed into a top scorer alongside Ilya Kovalchuk, Jarome Iginla, and Rick Nash. He scored 50 goals in each of his first two seasons with the Senators, eclipsing the 100-point mark both times as well, the only player in the league to achieve both these landmarks in their first two seasons. These were also team records for the Senators. More importantly, he took the team to the Stanley Cup finals in 2007, where they lost to Anaheim in five games.

The next two seasons saw a slight decline in production as his playing time was reduced, so Heatley asked to be traded and his request was granted. He touched down in San Jose in the fall of 2009, and immediately formed a high-scoring line with Patrick Marleau and Joe Thornton. Such was their success that Team Canada executive director Steve Yzerman selected all three players to the team for Vancouver.

Of course, Heatley's international resume is outstanding, culminating with back-to-back gold medals in the 2003 and 2004 World Championships, three other silver medals at the Worlds, and a victory in the finals of the 2004 World Cup of Hockey. He was also named tournament MVP at the World in both 2004 and 2008. Heatley is the all-time leader in goals (38) and points (62) at the World Championship.

INTERNATIONAL STATISTICS								
			GP	G	A	P	Pim	Place
2000	U20	CAN	7	2	2	4	4	B
2001	U20	CAN	7	3	2	5	10	B
2002	WM	CAN	7	2	2	4	2	6th
2003	WM	CAN	9	7	3	10	10	G
2004	WM	CAN	9	8	3	11	4	G
2004	WCH	CAN	6	0	2	2	2	1st
2005	WM	CAN	9	3	4	7	16	S
2006	OG	CAN	6	2	1	3	8	7th
2008	WM	CAN	9	12	8	20	4	S
2009	WM	CAN	9	6	4	10	8	S

IGINLA, JAROME

ST. ALBERT, ALBERTA,
JULY 1, 1977

RIGHT WING

SHOOTS RIGHT

6'1" 207 LBS

NHL TEAM: CALGARY FLAMES

CANADA

One of the toughest competitors and classiest players ever to play the game, Jarome Iginla can look to another Olympics (2002) as the tournament that changed him. Before that Gold-medal winning event, he was a rising star of whom great things were expected. After Salt Lake, he was expected to be a leader and superstar. And he delivered.

Iginla was drafted 11th overall by Dallas in 1995, but before he had a chance to play for the Stars he was traded, with Corey Millen, for Joe Nieuwendyk midway through the 1995–96 season while he was still in Kamloops. Although Iginla played two games in the 1996 playoffs (scoring his first NHL goal), it wasn't until the next fall that he made the team full time. He scored 21 goals as a rookie and proved to be just as fast and physical as much older players. It was clear he would be the cornerstone of the team for years to come. The team missed the playoffs, so he played for Canada at the World Championship, winning gold.

After a slightly disappointing sophomore year, Iginla had seasons of 28, 29, and 31 goals, and midway through the 2001–02 season he was named to Canada's Olympic team for Salt Lake. He was 24 years old, and the situation couldn't have been better for him because the team was led by executive director Wayne Gretzky, captain Mario Lemieux, Scott Niedermayer, and other players who had a much more commanding presence. Iginla could play his game without worry about pressure or expectations.

Of course, he took full advantage of the opportunity, scoring two goals in the Gold-medal game to help Canada to Gold for the first time in half a century. He returned to the Flames a more confident player and ended up leading the league in goals (with 52) to win the Rocket Richard Trophy and points (96) to win the Art Ross Trophy. He also won the Lester B. Pearson Award.

Ever since, Iginla has never failed to score at least 35 goals. He was named team captain in 2003 and has worn the "C" ever since. The Flames have become his team to lead. He shared a second Rocket Richard Trophy in 2003–04 when his 41 goals was tops in the league alongside Rick Nash and Ilya Kovalchuk.

Iginla played on the victorious 2004 World Cup of Hockey team and was named to Canada's 2006 Olympic team which finished a disappointing seventh. Now a veteran at 32, he comes to Vancouver as a leader, not a follower. The next generation will look up to him for inspiration and direction.

INTERNATIONAL STATISTICS			GP	G	A	P	Pim	Place
1996	U20	CAN	6	5	7	12	4	G
1997	WM	CAN	11	2	3	5	2	G
2002	OG	CAN	6	3	1	4	0	G
2004	WCH	CAN	6	2	1	3	2	1st
2006	OG	CAN	6	2	1	3	4	7th

KEITH, DUNCAN

WINNIPEG, MANITOBA, JULY 16, 1983

DEFENCE

SHOOTS LEFT

6'1" 194 LBS

NHL TEAM: **CHICAGO BLACKHAWKS**

A peripatetic childhood has given way to NHL stability for Duncan Keith who was born in Winnipeg, spent his early years in Fort Frances, Ontario, and then lived as a teen in Penticton, British Columbia. Even then, he moved to Michigan at age 18 to start a college career, and his path to the NHL.

Keith played in the historic "Cold War" outdoor game between Michigan and Michigan State (his alma mater) which set an attendance record for a hockey game at the start of the 2001–02 season. He played only a year and a half, however, before moving home and continuing his career in junior hockey with the Kelowna Rockets of the WHL, an increasingly common choice for young Canadian players.

Chicago had drafted Keith in 2002, and after just half a season in the WHL they assigned him to their AHL farm team in Norfolk for the start of the 2003–04 season. He spent two full years away from the glare of the NHL, developing into a reliable defenceman with and without the puck. By 2005, he was ready to play a role with the Hawks, and he has responded with remarkable success.

Perhaps the two stats which best illustrate Keith's swift rise are his ice time and plus-minus rating. As a rookie, he led all Hawks players with an average of more than 23 minutes a game, and this number has risen over the four years he has been with the team. At the same time, he was a -11 in plus/minus as a rookie, but in 2008–09 that number had risen sharply to a +33, when he was averaging a staggering 25:34 of ice time per game.

After his rookie season, the Hawks signed Keith to a five-year contract extension, but they had even bigger things in mind once they saw how great a player he was. In December 2009, they tore up this contract and drafted a new one which included 13 years and $72 million. Keith signed on the dotted line and, if all goes according to plan, the once travel-weary player will have spent his entire career in one place—Chicago.

Keith's only previous international experience with Team Canada came at the 2008 World Championship in Quebec City, the 100th anniversary of the IIHF. The Hawks failed to make the playoffs that year, and Keith jumped at the opportunity to wear a maple leaf sweater. The team made it to the gold-medal game before losing to Russia 4–3 in overtime.

INTERNATIONAL STATISTICS			GP	G	A	P	Pim	Place
2008 WM		CAN	9	0	2	2	6	S

LUONGO, ROBERTO

MONTREAL, QUEBEC,
APRIL 4, 1979

GOALIE

CATCHES LEFT

6'3" 205 LBS

NHL TEAM: VANCOUVER CANUCKS

It's hard to believe that's it's been nearly 13 years since Roberto Luongo was drafted 4th overall by the New York Islanders in 1997. The Islanders were not a quality team at the time, and they also believed that Rick DiPietro would become a better goalie. As a result, they traded Luongo after only 24 games to Florida. It was the best thing that could have happened to him. The Panthers were in need of a top goalie, and Luongo quickly developed into a star, posting a 2.44 goals-against average in 2000–01 despite having a record of 12–24–7 with the Panthers.

Luongo remained with the Panthers for five years, each feeling a lot like the previous one. He usually led the league in shots faced, had a great GAA and save percentage, but had a poor won-loss record because the Panthers lacked solid defence and scoring. Indeed, it wasn't until 2006 when he was traded that he got into his first playoff game. Previously, though, Luongo had proved himself internationally. The Panthers' poor play in the regular season meant he could represent Canada at the World Championship, and he won consecutive gold medals with Canada in 2003 and 2004, followed by a silver in 2005.

It was in Vancouver that Luongo blossomed and received much-deserved publicity. His play was what the fans hoped it would be, and at the end of his first season he had posted a record of 47–22–6, one win shy of the record set by Martin Brodeur. Additionally, Luongo was nominated for three of the game's most prestigious individual awards—Hart Trophy, Lester B. Pearson Award, and Vezina Trophy—although he finished second on each ballot.

The Canucks struggled in 2008–09 and Luongo started the final 31 games of the season in an effort to qualify for the playoffs. The team fell just short, but prior to the new year Luongo was named captain, an honour last bestowed upon a goalie in 1947–48 when Bill Durnan of Montreal served the role (it had been outlawed by the league, so skaters had to be responsible for talking to officials).

Although the team has yet to go deep into the playoffs, it expects Luongo to take them there. Prior to the start of the current 2009–10 season, he signed a 12-year, $64-million contract extension with the Canucks, ensuring he finishes his career with the team.

			GP	W-T-L	Mins	GA	SO	GAA	A	Pim	Place
INTERNATIONAL STATISTICS											
1998	U20	CAN	3	0-0-2	145:02	8	0	3.31	0	2	8th
1999	U20	CAN	7	4-1-2	405:13	13	2	1.92	1	0	S
2001	WM	CAN	2	2-0-0	83:36	2	0	1.44	0	0	5th
2003	WM	CAN	4	4-0-0	211:50	7	1	1.98	0	0	G
2004	WM	CAN	7	5-1-1	440:00	17	1	2.32	0	0	G
2004	WCH	CAN	1	1-0-0	63:45	3	0	2.82	0	0	1st
2005	WM	CAN	2	1-1-0	120:00	3	1	1.50	0	0	S
2006	OG	CAN	2	1-0-1	118:58	3	0	1.51	0	0	7th

MARLEAU, PATRICK

ANEROID, SASKATCHEWAN,
SEPTEMBER 15, 1979

CENTRE

SHOOTS LEFT

6'2" 220 LBS

NHL TEAM: SAN JOSE SHARKS

A big man with soft hands, Patrick Marleau has developed into one of the league's top scorers with San Jose, playing on a line with Joe Thornton and Dany Heatley. Ironically, Thornton was selected 1st overall in the 1997 Entry Draft and Marleau was selected 2nd by the Sharks, the team for which he has played his entire 12 years in the league.

Because he was such a skilled player even as a teen, Marleau left Seattle in the WHL to play with San Jose in the fall of 1997 when he was barely 18 years old. He had but 13 goals as a rookie, but showed tremendous promise, and slowly but surely everything about his game improved. He became a better passer, played better defensively, became a stronger leader, but the Sharks were frequently eliminated from the playoffs earlier than many expected.

Indeed, they didn't win a playoff series until 2001–02, Marleau's fifth season, after losing in the first round in each previous year. Marleau began the 2003–04 season as one of the team's rotating captains, but by the midway point everyone agreed he should assume the captaincy full time. He had won a gold medal with Canada at the World Championship, his first in three tries, but after 2003–04 he sat out a year during the lockout.

Marleau's career received an extra kick midway through 2005–06 when the team acquired Joe Thornton from Boston. The two played on a line together, and Thornton became a vital set-up man for the trigger happy Marleau. When Heatley came on board in 2009, the highest-scoring line in the league was born. Team Canada's executive director, Steve Yzerman, had little difficulty choosing the entire line to play in Vancouver. The only thing left for Marleau to do now is take the Sharks deep into the playoffs. Their best run came in 2003–04 when they advanced to the Conference finals, only to lose to Calgary in six games.

INTERNATIONAL STATISTICS			GP	G	A	P	Pim	Place
1999	WM	CAN	7	1	1	2	0	4th
2001	WM	CAN	7	2	3	5	4	5th
2003	WM	CAN	9	0	4	4	4	G
2005	WM	CAN	9	2	2	4	4	S

MORROW, BRENDEN

CARLYLE, SASKATCHEWAN,
JANUARY 16, 1979

LEFT WING

SHOOTS LEFT

5'11" 205 LBS

NHL TEAM: DALLAS STARS

CANADA

An exceptional two-way player with both skill and grit, Brenden Morrow took the Portland Winter Hawks to the Memorial Cup in 1998, the year after he was drafted by the Dallas Stars 25th overall. He played his final season of junior the following year, winning a silver medal with Canada at the World Junior Championship. He then joined the Stars.

Dallas had won the Stanley Cup the previous year, and with Morrow's help the team made it back to the Cup finals in 2000 as well. Unfortunately, they lost to New Jersey, and the team hasn't been back since.

Not the biggest player, Morrow relies on solid play at both ends of the ice for his success. He is certainly capable of scoring, but his defensive work is also stellar, and he has been a minus player in the plus-minus rating only twice in his career (and even then barely—a -2 in 2006–07 and -4 in 2008–09). He has also never failed to score at least 14 goals in any full season, although he has missed large portions of two seasons because of injury.

In December 2006, he suffered severed tendons in his wrist after being stepped on during a game, and in November 2008 he suffered a serious ACL injury to his right knee and missed the rest of the season, having played only 18 games. He returned in 2009–10, though, to play at his highest level, and was named to Team Canada on New Year's Eve, 2009.

Most famous among Morrow's achievements in the NHL was the night of May 5, 2008, when he scored in the fourth overtime to eliminate the San Jose Sharks and advance the Stars to the Western Conference finals. Internationally, he has played for Canada at four World Championships, winning gold in 2004 and silver the next year. He also appeared briefly at the 2004 World Cup for Canada.

INTERNATIONAL STATISTICS			GP	G	A	P	Pim	Place
1999	U20	CAN	7	1	7	8	4	S
2001	WM	CAN	1	0	0	0	0	5th
2002	WM	CAN	7	0	1	1	2	6th
2004	WM	CAN	9	0	3	3	12	G
2004	WCH	CAN	1	0	0	0	4	1st
2005	WM	CAN	9	0	1	1	6	S

NASH, RICK

BRAMPTON, ONTARIO,
JUNE 16, 1984

LEFT WING

SHOOTS LEFT

6'4" 218 LBS

NHL TEAM: COLUMBUS BLUE JACKETS

CANADA

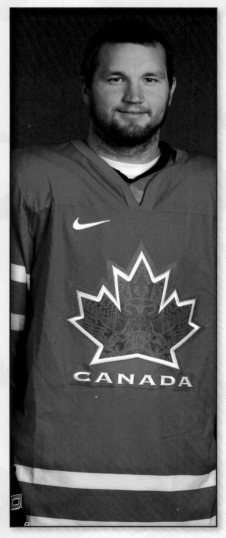

A pure goalscorer if ever there was one, Rick Nash has been a frequent and faithful representative of Canada on the international stage since he played at the World Junior Championship some eight years ago. Soon after winning a silver medal with that team in 2002, Columbus selected him 1st overall at the Entry Draft, and he made his NHL debut by scoring a goal later that fall.

Nash, like so many other players on Canada's Olympic team in Vancouver, is big and strong and is not easily moved off the puck. He had 17 goals as a rookie and was runner-up to Barret Jackman of St. Louis for the Calder Trophy. The next year he shared the Rocket Richard Trophy with Jarome Iginla and Ilya Kovalchuk, and, at 19 years of age, Nash became the youngest player in NHL history to lead the league in goals.

During his third season, the NHL lockout forced the cancellation of the entire year, so he and Joe Thornton played in the Swiss league for Davos, bringing the league championship to the team. After that victory, the pair stayed in Europe and played for Canada at the World Championship, winning silver after losing to the Czechs, 3–0, in the gold-medal game. Nash led the tournament in goals.

Despite an ankle injury the following year, Nash was still named to Canada's Olympic team for Turin. A year later, he again played for Canada, this time at the World Championship in Moscow. Canada won gold by beating Finland in the finals, and Nash scored the final goal of the event to clinch top spot with a sensational rush the length of the ice and deking the goalie while fighting off a Finnish player draped all over him.

In 2007–08, Nash scored a career best 38 goals, but one in particular stood out. On January 17, 2008, in the dying minutes against Phoenix, Nash deked two Coyote defenders with sensational moves, and then beat the goalie to give the Blue Jackets the win. It was hailed as the best goal of the season and replayed all over the world.

At season's end, he again played for Canada at the World Championship, this year held in Quebec City in honour of the IIHF's 100th anniversary. The team made it to the gold-medal game against Russia, but lost, 5–4, on an Ilya Kovalchuk overtime goal with Nash in the penalty box serving a delay-of-game penalty.

Soon after, he was named Columbus captain, and a year after that he signed an eight-year, $62.4-million contract extension. Nash is the face of the team, having spent all his seven NHL seasons with the Jackets, but the one thing that's lacking is playoff success. The team has been to the post-season only once, in 2009, where it was swept aside by Detroit in the first round.

INTERNATIONAL STATISTICS							
			GP	G	A	P	Pim	Place
2002 U20	CAN	7	1	2	3	2	S
2005 WM	CAN	9	9	6	15	8	S
2006 OG	CAN	6	0	1	1	10	7th
2007 WM	CAN	9	6	5	11	4	G
2008 WM	CAN	9	6	7	13	6	S

NIEDERMAYER, SCOTT

EDMONTON, ALBERTA,
AUGUST 31, 1973

DEFENCE

SHOOTS LEFT

6'1" 195 LBS

NHL TEAM: **ANAHEIM DUCKS**

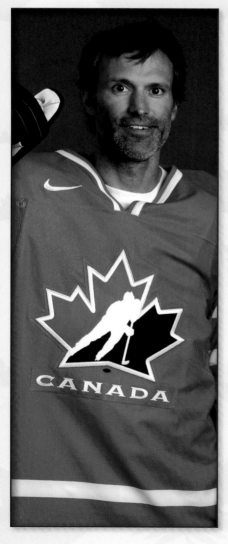

A winner at every level he's ever competed at, Scott Niedermayer is one of the finest defenceman hockey has ever known. One in a line of defenceman from Bobby Orr to Paul Coffey, he is a powerful skater with a smooth stride, an offensive player from the blue line who can dictate the pace of any game in which he plays.

Niedermayer was drafted 3rd overall by New Jersey in 1991 and made his debut with the Devils later that 1991–92 season. He graduated from Kamloops of the WHL where he won the Memorial Cup in the CHL and gold at the World Junior Championship, his first two titles of many honours. He spent the first 13 years of his career in New Jersey, helping the team go from being one of the worst teams in the league to the best. Alongside teammates such as goalie Martin Brodeur and Hall-of-Famer Scott Stevens, he was part of the team's first Stanley Cup win in 1995, when the Devils swept Detroit in a four-game finals.

New Jersey won the Cup again in 2000 and 2003, Niedermayer playing an evermore prominent role as he matured and gained experience. He played for Canada at the senior level for the first time at the 1996 World Cup of Hockey, but Canada finished a disappointing runner-up to the United States. Niedermayer was named to the Canadian Olympic team for 2002, and it was there he got a measure of comeuppance, helping Canada win Gold for the first time in 50 years.

New Jersey was eliminated in just five games from the 2004 playoffs, although the season had been hugely successful for him personally. He was named captain after Stevens was sidelined for a lengthy time because of injury, and he was named winner of the Norris Trophy for the first time. Because of the early playoff exit, he accepted an invitation to play for Canada at the World Championship in Czech Republic, an offer made sweeter by the knowledge his younger brother, Rob, was also going.

The entire Neidermayer family converged in Prague and watched the brothers win gold. Later that year, Scott again played for Canada at the World Cup, this time emerging victorious after facing the Finns in the finals. When he was named to the 2010 Olympic team, Niedermayer was also immediately named captain, owing to his experience and success at both the NHL and international level.

INTERNATIONAL STATISTICS			GP	G	A	P	Pim	Place
1991	U20	CAN	3	0	0	0	0	G
1992	U20	CAN	7	0	0	0	10	6th
1996	WCH	CAN	8	1	3	4	6	2nd
2002	OG	CAN	6	1	1	2	4	G
2004	WM	CAN	9	3	2	5	12	G
2004	WCH	CAN	6	1	1	2	9	1st

PERRY, COREY

PETERBOROUGH, ONTARIO,
MAY 16, 1985

RIGHT WING

SHOOTS RIGHT

6'3" 209 LBS

NHL TEAM: ANAHEIM DUCKS

One of the most talented young players in the game today, Corey Perry is becoming an NHL superstar at the exact moment he's playing on the international stage for the first time at such a high level. Perry brings with him a resume of high quality all the same.

Drafted 28th overall in 2003 by Anaheim, he was a big and strong player who needed more time to mature before he was ready for the NHL. The Ducks put no pressure on him, telling him to return to junior and enjoy himself—and that's exactly what he did. He played for London in the OHL, and in 2003–04 he led the league in assists and was one of the top scorers as well. The year after, he had the best junior career a teen could hope for.

For starters, he played for Canada at the World Junior Championship, winning gold while playing on a line with Sidney Crosby and Patrice Bergeron. He then led the OHL in goals (47), assists (83), and, of course, points (130), and then took the Knights to victory in the Memorial Cup where he was named tournament MVP. At 20 years old, he was finished with junior hockey and ready for the NHL.

There were few better places to begin a career than Anaheim at the time, as it had a team ready to compete for the Stanley Cup. Perry split the season between the Ducks (56 games) and the AHL affiliate in Portland (19 games). The year after he was with the Ducks full time. They went all the way in 2007, beating Ottawa in five games to win the Cup for the first time.

After that, Perry continued to blossom. He scored 29 goals and 54 points in 2007–08, and had 32 goals and 72 points the year after, becoming one of the leaders on a re-building team. That he was named to Canada's 2010 Olympic team, therefore, came as a surprise to no one.

INTERNATIONAL STATISTICS			GP	G	A	P	Pim	Place
2005	U20	CAN	6	2	5	7	6	G

PRONGER, CHRIS

DRYDEN, ONTARIO,
OCTOBER 10, 1974

DEFENCE

SHOOTS LEFT

6'6" 210 LBS

NHL TEAM: PHILADELPHIA FLYERS

The only Canadian to have appeared in all four Olympics since NHLers have been allowed to participate, Chris Pronger is also a member of the IIHF's prestigious Triple Gold Club.

The history books will forever show that Pronger was selected 2nd overall by Hartford in the 1993 Entry Draft soon after leading Peterborough to a Memorial Cup. Alexandre Daigle was chosen 1st overall by Ottawa in that draft, but history also shows that while Daigle vanished from the NHL map quickly, Pronger has become one of the most dominant defencemen of the modern era.

He first came to international prominence at the 1993 World Junior (U20) Championship as a member of the gold-medal team. It was to be Canada's first of five straight gold medals at this event, but Pronger graduated to the NHL the next season and never looked back.

A giant on the blue line, Pronger took a while to mature physically and emotionally, but under the tutelage of coach Mike Keenan he became one of the best players in the game. Pronger played two years with the Whalers before being traded to Keenan's St. Louis Blues, and it was there he stayed for nine years, becoming a fierce presence in front of his own goal as well as an impressive offensive force at the other end of the ice.

Pronger won his first Triple Gold Club honour at the 1997 World Championship, with Canada. The Blues had been ousted by Detroit in six games in the first round of the playoffs, and so Pronger headed to Helsinki along with Jarome Iginla and Anson Carter, among others. Canada beat Sweden 2–1 in the deciding game of a best-of-three finals, and Pronger was on his way to Triple-Gold-Club glory.

In the prime of his career, Pronger won both the Norris and Hart Trophies in 1999–2000, the first defenceman to do so since Bobby Orr in 1971–72. A year and a half later, he was one of the anchors of Canada's Olympic team which won Gold at Salt Lake.

After the lockout, Pronger signed with Edmonton and had an immediate impact. The Oilers went to the Stanley Cup finals before losing to Carolina in game seven, after which he asked for a trade. The team accommodated, and Pronger went to Anaheim to join Scott Niedermayer as the best one-two blue line combination in the NHL. Again, Pronger's impact was sensational, but this time the final game of the season ended in victory, not defeat. The Ducks beat Ottawa in five games and with the win, Pronger had now won all three honours associated with the Triple Gold Club.

INTERNATIONAL STATISTICS							
		GP	G	A	P	Pim	Place
1993 U20	CAN	7	1	3	4	6	G
1997 WM	CAN	9	0	2	2	12	G
1998 OG	CAN	6	0	0	0	4	4th
2002 OG	CAN	6	0	1	1	2	G
2006 OG	CAN	6	1	2	3	16	7th

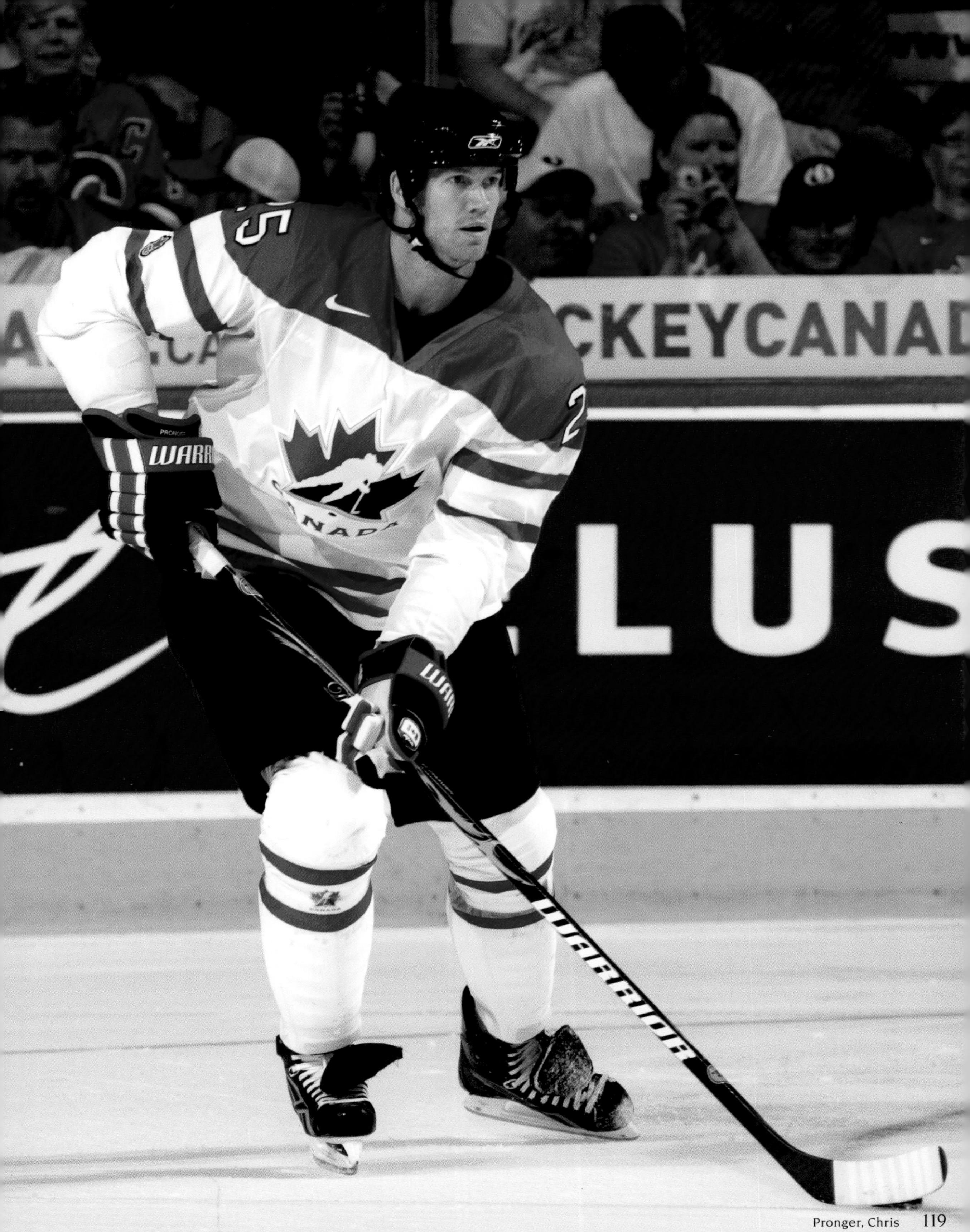
CKEYCANAD
LUS

RICHARDS, MIKE

KENORA, ONTARIO,
FEBRUARY 11, 1985

CENTRE

SHOOTS LEFT

5'11" 195 LBS

NHL TEAM: PHILADELPHIA FLYERS

It is without question the most difficult and rarest goal in hockey, but Mike Richards has done it three times. More than any player in NHL history, he has scored three goals while on a 3-on-5 situation. This alone attests to why he was chosen to play for Canada in 2010. Not only is he highly skilled in the offensive end, he is dangerous and effective as a checker and a penalty killer.

Richards was drafted by Philadelphia in 2003, 24th overall, while he was in mid-career with Kitchener in the OHL. Only weeks earlier he had led the Rangers to a Memorial Cup victory, and just before that he had won a gold medal with Canada at the 2005 World Junior Championship. Richards remained in junior until the end of the 2004–05 season at which time he joined the Flyers' AHL team, also located in Philadelphia, and helped them win a Calder Cup.

He joined the Flyers full time the next season and scored a goal in his first game, but perhaps more telling was his first hat trick. That came February 8, 2006, against the New York Islanders and included two short-handed goals. The next season he missed 23 games with stomach surgery and wasn't as effective as he knew he could be, but in 2007–08 he started to become a dominant figure not just on the team but among the league's elite.

In 73 games, he had 28 goals and 75 points to lead the team, but midway through, in December 2007, he signed a monster 12-year, $69-million contract extension, a clear sign that the Flyers wanted to build their team around him. In the 2008 playoffs, he continued his dominance, taking the Flyers to the Conference finals where they lost to state rivals, Pittsburgh.

At training camp leading into the 2008–09 season, Richards was named team captain. The 23-year-old then scored his third 3-on-5 goal to set a new NHL record, and he also scored short-handed goals in three consecutive games, a feat not achieved in the NHL in more than a decade. Again, though, the team fell to the Penguins in the playoffs, this time in the first round.

Richards immediately had left shoulder surgery for an ongoing problem and still requires surgery on his right shoulder, which he'll likely deal with in the off-season. Prior to this season, he had 18 career power-play goals and 19 career short-handed goals among the 79 he has scored in his brief career to date.

INTERNATIONAL STATISTICS							
		GP	G	A	P	Pim	Place
2004 U20	CAN	6	2	3	5	2	S
2005 U20	CAN	6	1	4	5	2	G
2006 WM	CAN	9	3	2	5	10	4th

SEABROOK, BRENT

RICHMOND, BRITISH COLUMBIA, APRIL 20, 1985

DEFENCE

SHOOTS RIGHT

6'3" 220 LBS

NHL TEAM: CHICAGO BLACKHAWKS

Incredibly, Brent Seabrook played minor hockey with a team called the Pacific Vipers in Tsawwassen, British Columbia, where three other future Chicago Blackhawks teammates played—Andrew Ladd, Troy Brouwer, and Colin Fraser. Seabrook was drafted by the Hawks 14th overall in 2003, after leading Canada to a gold medal at the World U18 Championship.

Although the defenceman was still two years away from joining the NHL, he made the most of his major junior career with Lethbridge, and Team Canada at the World Junior Championship, winning a silver and gold medal in successive seasons.

Seabrook made the Hawks at training camp in 2005 and has been a mainstay on the blue line ever since, averaging more than 20 minutes a game throughout his career. One of the more unsung players on Canada's 2010 team, he has partnered so effectively with Duncan Keith in Chicago that executive director Steve Yzerman decided to name both players to the Olympic team for Vancouver. The pair complement each other perfectly and, given their experience as a team, it only made sense to bring them to a short tournament such as the Olympics where communication and cohesion are major factors for success.

Playing in Vancouver adds a final level of accomplishment to the Seabrook resume, as he has now played for Canada at every major IIHF tournament: U18, the World Juniors, the World Championship, and, now, the Olympics. Although he is blessed with some ability in the offensive zone, he is known more for his superb work inside his own blue line, limiting scoring chances and moving the puck up ice quickly and effectively.

INTERNATIONAL STATISTICS							
			GP	G	A	P	Pim	Place
2003	U18	CAN	7	3	3	6	4	G
2004	U20	CAN	6	1	2	3	2	S
2005	U20	CAN	5	0	3	3	0	G
2006	WM	CAN	8	0	0	0	2	4th

STAAL, ERIC

THUNDER BAY, ONTARIO,
OCTOBER 29, 1984

CENTRE

SHOOTS LEFT

6'4" 205 LBS

NHL TEAM: CAROLINA HURRICANES

Few players in the hockey world have accomplished as much by age 24 as Eric Staal, one of four hockey-playing brothers brought up on the family farm near Thunder Bay, Ontario.

Staal was drafted by Carolina 2nd overall in 2003 behind only Marc-Andre Fleury, and he made the team that fall, at 18 years old. He had played three seasons with the Peterborough Petes in the OHL but was clearly ready to move on after his final season.

Big, but a graceful stickhandler, Staal was effective with the puck and without it. He protected it well, making it difficult at best to knock him off stride, moving into the opening as well as any teenager. He missed only a single game that rookie season, and thereafter played every game for the next four years, a clear sign of his "Iron Man" status.

The Hurricanes surprised the hockey world in 2005–06 by winning the Stanley Cup in Staal's second season. As a rookie he had eleven goals and 31 points, but that year he had 45 goals and 100 points, and it was his swift development that was a key part of the team's great playoff success. Indeed, he led all scorers in the post season in assists (19) and points (28), although goalie Cam Ward won the Conn Smythe Trophy.

The Hurricanes failed to make the playoffs the next year, but this allowed him to play for Canada at the World Championship in Russia. Even better, his brother Jordan, from Pittsburgh, also played, and the pair led Canada to a gold medal.

Staal hasn't replicated those amazing NHL stats from that Cup year, but he has also never failed to score at least 30 goals or 70 points. He was named MVP of the 2008 All-Star Game in Atlanta, and that fall, he signed a seven-year $57.75-million contract extension with the team.

On January 10, 2010, Staal was named team captain in place of Rod Brind'Amour, making official what fans and everyone in the organization had known for some time. Eric Staal is the most important player on the Hurricanes.

INTERNATIONAL STATISTICS							
2002 U18	CAN	8	2	5	7	4	6th
2007 WM	CAN	9	5	5	10	6	G
2008 WM	CAN	8	4	3	7	6	S

THORNTON, JOE

LONDON, ONTARIO,
JULY 2, 1979

CENTRE

SHOOTS LEFT

6'4" 235 LBS

NHL TEAM: SAN JOSE SHARKS

One of the most effective power forwards in the game today, Joe Thornton is the perfect example of a big man who took a while to get going. But since he's gotten up and running, few have been able to stop him. He was drafted 1st overall in 1997 by Boston, and when he joined the Bruins at his first training camp that fall, he was expected to make an immediate impact at just 18 years old.

In reality, he attracted little attention, scoring just three goals and four assists in a whopping 55 games. Another Boston rookie, Sergei Samsonov, won the Calder Trophy and was making Thornton look like a poor first overall selection. But Thornton stuck with his game, learned the league, its tricks, his opponents, and he improved quickly. By his fourth year, he had 37 goals and 107 points, and talk of him being a disappointment was no more.

It was his first of four seasons of at least 98 points, and he lost little steam in 2004–05 during the lockout when he played in Switzerland. Davos was the beneficiary, as Thornton and Rick Nash helped the team win the Swiss championship. At the end of the season, they both joined Team Canada for the World Championship, winning a silver medal.

But the Bruins had had a series of early playoff exits despite Thornton's great regular seasons, and early in 2005–06 they traded him to San Jose for Marco Sturm, Brad Stuart, and Wayne Primeau. Thornton found new life on the west coast, often playing with Patrick Marleau, and that trade year saw him become the first player to win the Art Ross Trophy playing for two teams. He added to his collection by winning the Hart Trophy, further salt in the wound of Bruins management for trading him away.

Thornton has been the cornerstone of the team ever since. He is a passer first and scorer second, using his incredible strength and size to shield the puck, barge to the crease, and make a quick pass. It was largely his play which allowed teammate Jonathan Cheechoo to win the Rocket Richard Trophy in 2005–06, the most unlikely scoring leader in many years. Prior to this 2009–10 season, Thornton had 842 points in 836 career games, but this point-a-game average yielded only 265 goals. The lesson linemates have learned is, go to the net, stick on the ice, and Big Joe will get you the puck.

INTERNATIONAL STATISTICS							
		GP	G	A	P	Pim	Place
1997 U20	CAN	7	2	2	4	0	G
2001 WM	CAN	6	1	1	2	6	5th
2004 WCH	CAN	6	1	5	6	0	1st
2005 WM	CAN	9	6	10	16	4	S
2006 OG	CAN	6	1	2	3	0	7th

TOEWS, JONATHAN

WINNIPEG, MANITOBA,
APRIL 29, 1988

CENTRE

SHOOTS LEFT

6'2" 209 LBS

NHL TEAM: CHICAGO BLACKHAWKS

Although Jonathan Toews won gold with Canada's juniors in 2006, he was a 17-year-old who was there more for the experience than as a player Team Canada was counting on. Not so the next year when he had one of the most memorable games in World Junior Championship history. In the semifinals, Canada faced arch-rivals, the United States, and after 60 minutes of regulation and ten minutes of overtime, the game was still tied. Thus, a shootout was necessary.

Toews beat goalie Jeffrey Frazee during the opening round, but this was tied 2–2, so sudden death shots were needed. Coach Craig Hartsburg returned to Toews after one failed round, and Toews scored again. So did the Americans. Another scoreless round had Hartsburg calling Toews's name for a third time, and for a third time Toews scored. This time, Carey Price made one final save, and Canada went on to win the gold medal, all thanks to Toews's record three shootout goals in one game.

Later that season, he became one of a rare group of players to represent Canada at the World Championship without having NHL experience, and he completed an even rarer double by becoming the first Canadian to win gold at the World Junior and senior Championships in the same season.

That anecdote points to the poise and maturity of the young player who had been drafted 3rd overall the previous year by Chicago. Toews finished his second year at North Dakota and then joined the Hawks as a rookie for the 2007–08 season at age 20. On October 10, 2007, Toews scored a goal on his first shot in his first NHL game, and went on to record points in his first ten NHL games, the second-longest such streak in league history.

After a rookie season in which he scored 24 goals and 54 points in just 64 games, Toews was runner-up to teammate Patrick Kane in Calder Trophy voting (Kane played all 82 games and had 72 points). That summer, at age 20, Toews was named team captain of the Hawks, the third youngest in league history after Vincent Lecavalier and Sidney Crosby. In his second season on a rebuilding Chicago team, Toews had 34 goals and took the Hawks to the Conference finals in the playoffs before losing to Detroit in five games.

INTERNATIONAL STATISTICS			GP	G	A	P	Pim	Place
2006	U20	CAN	6	0	2	2	2	G
2007	U20	CAN	6	4	3	7	12	G
2007	WM	CAN	9	2	5	7	6	G
2008	WM	CAN	9	2	3	5	8	S

WEBER, SHEA

SICAMOUS, BRITISH COLUMBIA, AUGUST 14, 1985

DEFENCE

SHOOTS RIGHT

6'4" 230 LBS

NHL TEAM: NASHVILLE PREDATORS

Another 24-year-old on the team, Shea Weber is a big, strong defenceman who came out of that exceptional 2003 draft year. In his case, he was selected by Nashville 49th overall while playing for the Kelowna Rockets of the WHL. During his junior days, he played for Canada at the 2005 World Junior Championship, playing on one of the greatest junior teams of all time.

After graduating from junior, he turned pro in 2005 and divided his first season between the Predators and their AHL affiliate in Milwaukee. Interestingly, he played in both the regular season and playoffs for both Nashville and Milwaukee, appearing in a total of 92 games that season. He has been with Nashville full time since 2006, quietly making his way to the top of the rankings of defencemen for his combination of speed, physical play, and surprising offensive ability.

Weber's second full season was punctuated by two injuries. He dislocated his kneecap in his first game, the season opener, missing six weeks, and later he hurt his leg and missed another eleven games. His breakout season came in 2008–09 when he played 81 of the 82 games on the schedule and scored 23 goals, among the league leaders in this category for defencemen. As well, he has become one of those workhorse defencemen a team covets, playing 24 minutes a game and maintaining a respectable plus-minus rating on a mediocre team.

Indeed, that has been the biggest downfall to Weber's early years so far. The Predators have made the playoffs three of four years he's been in the league but have won a total of just three games. On the positive side, these early playoff exits have allowed him to play for Canada at the World Championship. Twice he has played overseas, winning a gold medal in 2007 and a silver medal two years later.

INTERNATIONAL STATISTICS			GP	G	A	P	Pim	Place
2005	U20	CAN	6	0	0	0	10	G
2007	WM	CAN	6	1	1	2	31	G
2009	WM	CAN	9	4	8	12	6	S

WOMEN'S TEAM, 2010

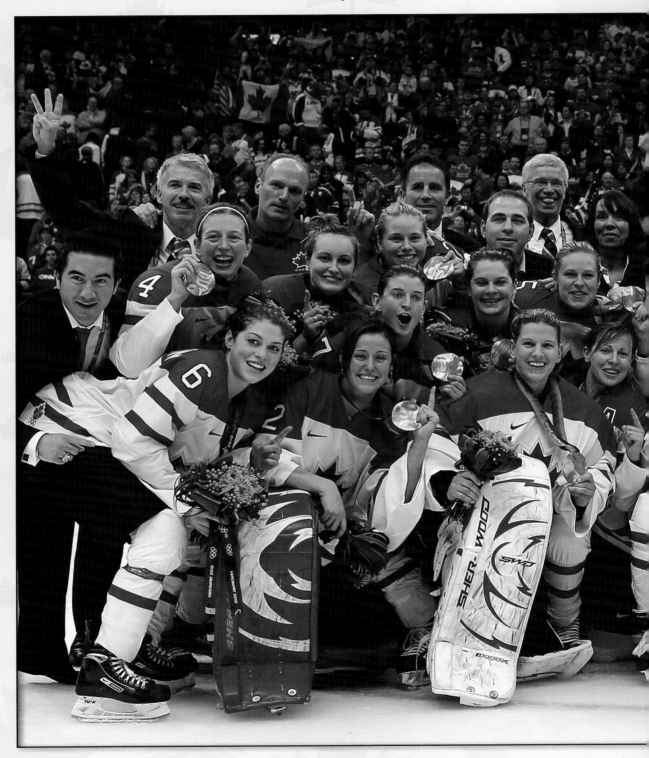

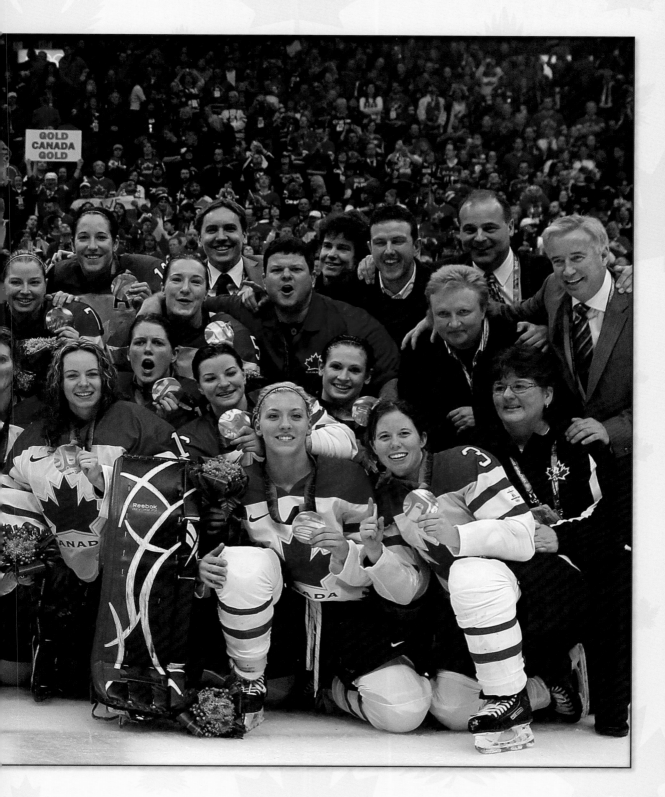

AGOSTA, MEGHAN

WINDSOR, ONTARIO, FEBRUARY 12, 1987

FORWARD

SHOOTS LEFT

5'7" 147 LBS

CLUB TEAM: **MERCYHURST COLLEGE, CHA**

Meghan Agosta had plenty of experience with Canada's U22 national team before she played at her first major event—the 2006 Olympics. She was with the U22 program from 2004 to 2009, acting as captain along the way. This experience overlapped with lesser senior playing time, notably at the 4 Nations Cup from 2004 to 2007.

In 2003, Agosta won a gold medal with Team Ontario at the Canada Winter Games, and two years later she helped Team Ontario Red win gold at the national U18 championship. An accomplished rollerblader as well, she scored the gold-medal goal for Canada at the 2004 World InLine Hockey Championship.

In 2006, Agosta enrolled at Mercyhurst College to major in criminal law, and is now in her senior year. Her achievements there have been legendary, beginning in her rookie season, 2006–07, when she was named CHA rookie of the year and player of the year as well as a short-listed finalist for the prestigious Patty Kazmaier Award. She took a break from school to participate in the Olympics, contributing three goals in Canada's run to Gold.

The next year she was CHA player of the year again and took the team to the league championship. In her third year, Agosta took Mercyhurst to the NCAA finals and was again shortlisted for the Kazmaier Award. She was the college's all-time leader in goals even before starting her senior year.

Agosta has played in all three World Women's Championships since Turin, and her participation in Vancouver marks her fifth straight major international tournament.

INTERNATIONAL STATISTICS							
		GP	G	A	P	Pim	Place
2006 OG-W	CAN	5	3	1	4	2	G
2007 WWC	CAN	5	0	4	4	4	G
2008 WWC	CAN	5	3	0	3	8	S
2009 WWC	CAN	5	2	2	4	2	S

APPS, GILLIAN

NORTH YORK (TORONTO), ONTARIO, NOVEMBER 2, 1983

FORWARD

SHOOTS LEFT

6' 177 LBS

CLUB TEAM: BRAMPTON CANADETTE-THUNDER, CWHL

When the senior women's team attended centralized training camp in the fall of 2001 to prepare for the 2002 Olympics, Gillian Apps was the youngest player there. She didn't make the team that time, but she did a year later for the 2003 World Women's Championship. Unfortunately, that event was cancelled because of the SARS outbreak, so Apps had to wait until 2004 to make her debut with the senior team. No matter. It seemed inevitable it would happen one day.

Apps is one of the most famous names in hockey. Gillian's dad played in the NHL for many years, and her grandfather was Hall-of-Famer and Stanley Cup champion Syl, who played for the Maple Leafs. Hockey, needless to say, is in her blood.

While she wasn't able to play at the 2003 WWC, Apps did enroll at Dartmouth College where she played for four years. She had an outstanding career and was named captain as a senior. She was named ECAC MVP for 2006–07 and was shortlisted for the Patty Kazmaier Award. After graduating, she returned home to play in the CWHL, leading Brampton to a championship in her first season, 2007–08.

Throughout her college years, Apps was a member of Team Canada's senior team. The highlight of her career came in 2006 when she was one of the dominant players at the Olympics and helped the country defend its gold medal title. Now a veteran of the team, she mentors the younger players, hoping to mould new champions.

INTERNATIONAL STATISTICS				GP	G	A	P	Pim	Place
2004	WWC	CAN		5	4	0	4	10	G
2005	WWC	CAN		5	4	2	6	8	S
2006	OG-W	CAN		5	7	7	14	14	G
2007	WWC	CAN		5	1	3	4	6	G
2008	WWC	CAN		5	1	0	1	8	S
2009	WWC	CAN		5	2	1	3	4	S

~Olympics All-Star team/Forward (2006)

BONHOMME, TESSA

SUDBURY, ONTARIO,
JULY 23, 1985

FORWARD

SHOOTS LEFT

5'7" 140 LBS

CLUB TEAM: CALGARY OVAL X-TREME, WWHL

Tessa Bonhomme has been a part of Canada's women's program since 2004, starting with the U22 team. Prior to that, she played for the Sudbury Lady Wolves in Intermediate AA hockey from 1998 to 2003, the same organization that current teammate Rebecca Johnston would join in 2004.

She played in an exhibition series against the United States and appeared in the Air Canada Cup for three successive years, 2005–07. Her rise to prominence was gradual. She was named an alternate for the 2005 World Women's Championship, and in 2006 she was among the group of 27 players who centralized in preparation for Turin. She didn't make the final roster, but she did make the grade a year later for the 2007 WWC.

Bonhomme left Sudbury in 2003 to attend Ohio State University where she majored in speech pathology. She was named rookie of the year for both the university and the WCHA and a year later was named Ohio State's most valuable player. She took a year off from the Buckeyes during 2005–06 in the hopes of making the Olympic team, but after that dream didn't come true she returned to the school to complete her education and continue her career with the hockey team. In 2007–08, her senior year, Bonhomme was not only team captain but a Patty Kazmaier Award finalist.

After graduating, she moved to Calgary and played for the Oval X-Treme of the WWHL, going as far as the semifinals of the 2009 Clarkson Cup.

INTERNATIONAL STATISTICS							
		GP	G	A	P	Pim	Place
2007 WWC	CAN	5	1	1	2	6	G
2009 WWC	CAN	5	0	3	3	0	S

BOTTERILL, JENNIFER

WINNIPEG, MANITOBA, MAY 1, 1979

FORWARD

SHOOTS LEFT

5'9" 158 LBS

CLUB TEAM: MISSISSAUGA CHIEFS, CWHL

Superior athletic ability runs in the Botterill family. Jennifer's mother, Doreen, was a member of Canada's speedskating team at the 1964 and 1968 Olympics while older brother Jason played in the NHL after winning a record three gold medals with Canada at the World Junior Championship. Not to be outdone, Jennifer is among the most successful and highly accomplished female hockey players of the modern era.

Botterill enrolled at Harvard University at age 19 in 1998, and over the next five years completed her degree while setting all-time records on ice that may never be beaten. She is the top scorer in NCAA history with 149 goals, 170 assists, and 319 total points in just 107 games.

In all, she was held pointless exactly once in her years at Harvard and set a record by registering a point in 80 consecutive games. Botterill is also the only woman to have won the Patty Kazmaier Award twice (2001 and 2003). In her rookie year she led the team to the NCAA championship while being named tournament MVP of the Frozen Four.

After graduating from Harvard, Botterill returned home to play in the CWHL, and she continued her scoring ways. In 2004–05, she helped the Toronto Aeros win the national championship, a feat she replicated in 2008 with the Mississauga Chiefs. She also led the CWHL in scoring that year.

Internationally, Botterill has enjoyed similar success, winning gold or silver in eleven Olympics and World Women's Championships combined. Her finest hour was at the 2001 WWC when she was named tournament MVP and best forward by the IIHF directorate, and led all players with eight goals in five games.

A gifted scorer and dominant presence on the ice, Botterill is an essential component of Team Canada.

INTERNATIONAL STATISTICS							
1998	OG-W	CAN	6	0	0	0	0	S
1999	WWC	CAN	5	1	3	4	0	G
2000	WWC	CAN	5	1	5	6	2	G
2001	WWC	CAN	5	8	2	10	4	G
2002	OG-W	CAN	5	3	3	6	8	G
2004	WWC	CAN	5	3	8	11	0	G
2005	WWC	CAN	5	1	6	7	4	S
2006	OG-W	CAN	5	1	6	7	4	G
2007	WWC	CAN	5	3	2	5	4	G
2008	WWC	CAN	5	4	4	8	4	S
2009	WWC	CAN	5	5	3	8	2	S

~World Women's Championship Tournament MVP (2001, 2004),
IIHF Directorate World Women's Championship best forward (2001),
World Women's Championship All-Star team/Forward (2004)

HEFFORD, JAYNA

TRENTON, ONTARIO,
MAY 14, 1977

FORWARD

SHOOTS LEFT

5'5" 138 LBS

CLUB
TEAM: BRAMPTON CANADETTE-THUNDER, CWHL

CANADA

Jayna Hefford has been playing serious hockey since 1994, but no moment can match the Gold-medal game of the 2002 Olympics in Salt Lake against the host nation. In a game marred by a succession of penalties to Canada, Hefford scored a goal with a single second left in the second period to give Canada a 3–1 lead. Although the Americans scored once in the third period, they couldn't tie the game and Hefford's goal turned out to be the winner.

Playing big in crucial games was nothing new for her. In the gold-medal game of the 2000 World Women's Championship, she scored twice in the final period against the US to send the game into overtime. Nancy Drolet then scored to give Canada the win.

Hefford played for Team Ontario at the U18 nationals in 1994 and was captain of her provincial team, winning the Canada Winter Games the following year. Soon after, she enrolled at the University of Toronto, and in 1997 she made her debut at the top level of play at the WWC. She has been with the senior national team ever since.

Hefford led the tournament in scoring at both the 1999 and 2000 WWC, helping Canada win gold both times. She was later named the best forward by the IIHF directorate at the 2004 and 2005 WWC and was named to the All-Star team three times.

In addition to her play with Team Canada, Hefford has been one of the longest-serving players in the NWHL/CWHL, starring with the Brampton Thunder and later Brampton Canadette-Thunder since 1998. She is the league's all-time leading scorer.

INTERNATIONAL STATISTICS								
			GP	G	A	P	Pim	Place
1997	WWC	CAN	5	1	3	4	2	G
1998	OG-W	CAN	6	1	0	1	6	S
1999	WWC	CAN	5	5	6	11	0	G
2000	WWC	CAN	5	5	3	8	4	G
2001	WWC	CAN	5	2	2	4	6	G
2002	OG-W	CAN	5	3	4	7	2	G
2004	WWC	CAN	5	7	3	10	2	G
2005	WWC	CAN	5	6	2	8	0	S
2006	OG-W	CAN	5	3	4	7	0	G
2007	WWC	CAN	5	2	1	3	2	G
2008	WWC	CAN	5	3	5	8	8	S
2009	WWC	CAN	5	1	6	7	2	S

~IIHF Directorate World Women's Championship best forward (2004, 2005), World Women's Championship All-Star team/Forward (1999, 2004, 2008)

IRWIN, HALEY

THUNDER BAY, ONTARIO, JUNE 6, 1988

FORWARD

SHOOTS LEFT

5'7" 172 LBS

CLUB TEAM: UNIVERSITY OF MINNESOTA-DULUTH, WCHA

It wasn't until she was 16 years old that Haley Irwin left boys hockey to play for Canada's U22 national team, but the early years with players bigger and stronger served her well later in her career. Irwin was the dominant player in OWHA play with the Toronto Jr. Aeros in both 2004–05 and 2005–06, and she participated in several national-level tournaments as well, winning gold with Team Ontario at the 2003 Canada Winter Games and the 2005 women's nationals.

Former Team Canada coach Shannon Miller, now at the University of Minnesota-Duluth, recruited Irwin for the team in the fall of 2007, but what had come easily to Irwin up to this point got more difficult at such a high level of play.

Miller spent time whipping Irwin into shape—physically and psychologically—and Irwin responded, leading the WCHA in scoring and being named rookie of the year. In the Frozen Four at the end of the year, it was Irwin's goal against Wisconsin that gave UMD the championship. A year later, the team made it to the semifinals before being eliminated.

Irwin had been a member of the national U22 team since 2007, playing various tournaments and exhibition games, but she made her senior debut at the 2009 World Women's Championship. Big and strong, she is a power forward and scorer on whom Canada relies for offense.

INTERNATIONAL STATISTICS						
	GP	G	A	P	Pim	Place
2009 WWC CAN	5	2	3	5	2	S

JOHNSTON, REBECCA

SUDBURY, ONTARIO,
SEPTEMBER 24, 1989

FORWARD

SHOOTS LEFT

5'7" 167 LBS

CLUB TEAM: CORNELL UNIVERSITY, ECAC

At 20 years old, Rebecca Johnston was the second youngest on the team for the 2010 Olympics, but even still she was a veteran of the national U22 team for three years when she made the jump to senior competition. Johnston played for Canada at the MLP/Air Canada Cup from 2007 to 2009 as well as several important exhibition series against the United States starting in 2006. In addition, she played at the 4 Nations Cup in both 2008 and 2009 in preparation for the World Women's Championships.

During her earlier days, Johnston played Intermediate AA hockey with the Sudbury Lady Wolves from 2004 to 2007. In 2005, she played for Team Ontario Red at the national U18 tournament and was named best forward and two years later led Team Ontario to gold at the Canada Winter Games.

Johnston started attending Cornell University in the fall of 2007. She led the team in goals and points and was named Ivy League rookie of the year at the end of her freshman season. A year later, faster and stronger, she was Cornell's MVP and a long list finalist for the Patty Kazmaier Award.

Johnston combines size and speed and has soft hands around the net. Still maturing and developing, she is a player to watch for years to come.

INTERNATIONAL STATISTICS						
	GP	G	A	P	Pim	Place
2008 WWC CAN	5	0	0	0	0	S
2009 WWC CAN	5	3	2	5	0	S

KELLAR, BECKY

HAGERSVILLE, ONTARIO, JANUARY 1, 1975

DEFENCE

SHOOTS LEFT

5'7" 146 LBS

CLUB TEAM: BURLINGTON BARRACUDAS, CWHL

One of the many multi-gold veterans of Canada's 2010 women's team, Becky Kellar has been one of the lynchpins of the defence for more than a decade. She made her international debut at the 1998 Olympics in Nagano after graduating from Brown University with a degree in psychology the previous year. At graduation she was awarded Academic All-Ivy status for her excellent combination of athletics and academics.

Kellar first rose to prominence at the national U18 championship in 1993, when she led Team Ontario to victory. She was named MVP of the gold-medal game that year and soon after attended Brown where she won numerous awards over her four-year career. In addition to playing hockey in the winter, Kellar also played for Brown's softball team for four years as a second baseman.

Beginning with Nagano, Kellar has played at every important tournament for Canada with the exception of the 2007 World Women's Championship. She had given birth to her second son that January, and took the year off to raise him. Her first child was born in October 2004, but the timing was such that she didn't miss any time with the national team.

Kellar is a defensive defenceman, not known for her scoring or skating but a gem inside her own blue line. She is one of a rare group to have played in all Olympics in which women have played, winning Gold in 2002 and 2006. She has won four gold medals at the World Women's Championship as well.

Outside of the national team, Kellar has played continuously in the NWHL and CWHL and has completed her MBA at Wilfred Laurier University.

INTERNATIONAL STATISTICS							
			GP	G	A	P	Pim	Place
1998	OG-W	CAN	6	1	2	3	2	S
1999	WWC	CAN	5	1	0	1	6	G
2000	WWC	CAN	5	2	2	4	0	G
2001	WWC	CAN	5	1	2	3	2	G
2002	OG-W	CAN	5	0	1	1	6	G
2004	WWC	CAN	4	0	0	0	0	G
2005	WWC	CAN	5	0	2	2	4	S
2006	OG-W	CAN	5	0	1	1	2	G
2008	WWC	CAN	5	1	4	5	0	S
2009	WWC	CAN	5	0	0	0	4	S

KINGSBURY, GINA

URANIUM CITY, SASKATCHEWAN,
NOVEMBER 26, 1981

FORWARD

SHOOTS LEFT

5'8" 137 LBS

CLUB TEAM: CALGARY OVAL X-TREME, WWHL

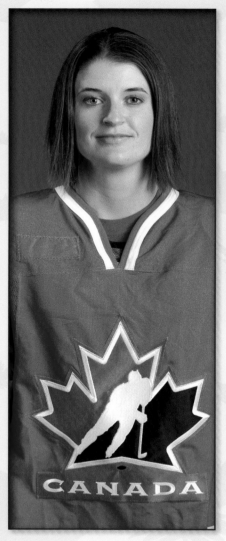

When she was just 13 years old, Gina Kingsbury played for Team Quebec at the Canada Winter Games, an event she returned to four years later at age 17. In between, she played for her province at the national U18 tournament in 1997, but in 2000, she enrolled at St. Lawrence and played the most serious hockey of her career.

That year, Kingsbury helped the team reach the Frozen Four for women's hockey before losing to powerhouse Minnesota-Duluth. She stayed the full four years, graduating with a degree in psychology. She was a First Team All-Star for the ECAC that year, after which she returned home to play in the NWHL and later in the WWHL. In 2004–05, she played for the Montreal Axion, after which she moved out west. In 2006–07, she and the Calgary X-Treme won the league championship and carried on to win the nationals, and she has continued to play with the X-Treme ever since.

Although she made her debut with the senior women's team a successful one by winning gold at the World Women's Championship in 2001, Kingsbury was a late cut from the Olympic team the following year. More determined than ever, she made sure never to be on the outside looking in, and she has established herself as a consistent representative ever since. Kingsbury was part of the historic 2006 Gold-medal team in Turin, and has won three WWC gold medals in all.

INTERNATIONAL STATISTICS							
			GP	G	A	P	Pim	Place
2001	WWC	CAN	4	2	2	4	0	G
2004	WWC	CAN	5	1	1	2	4	G
2005	WWC	CAN	5	2	0	2	4	S
2006	OG-W	CAN	5	0	3	3	2	G
2007	WWC	CAN	5	2	0	2	0	G
2008	WWC	CAN	5	1	3	4	0	S
2009	WWC	CAN	5	1	2	3	2	S

LABONTE, CHARLINE

GREENFIELD PARK, QUEBEC,
OCTOBER 15, 1982

GOALIE

CATCHES LEFT

5'9" 173 LBS

CLUB
TEAM: MCGILL UNIVERSITY, CIS

CANADA

Although she hasn't always been the team's number-one goalie, Charline Labonte has been an integral part of Team Canada for nearly a decade. After playing for Team Quebec at the 1999 Canada Winter Games, she played for Canada's U22 team for several years. She also became the second female after Manon Rheaume to play major junior hockey by appearing in several games for Acadie-Bathurst Titans of the QMJHL in 1999–2000.

Such was her reputation that Labonte was only 19 when she was named Canada's third goalie for the 2002 Olympics in Salt Lake City. She also filled this role in 2003 and 2004 at the World Women's Championship, patiently biding her time until she could make an appearance at the highest level of women's hockey.

In 2004–05, Labonte kept sharp by playing for the Montreal Axion in the NWHL, but she also played in four 4 Nations Cup tournaments, most notably in 2003 and 2004 when she was trying to establish herself on the senior national team.

Her chance finally came in 2005, during the WWC. In two games she didn't yield a single goal. At the 2006 Olympics, she shared the goaltending duties with Kim St. Pierre, and to the surprise of many it was Labonte who started in the Gold-medal game. Her Olympic Gold victory was the culmination of years of work and patience.

A teammate of Catherine Ward at McGill, Labonte backstopped the team to consecutive CIS national championships in 2008 and 2009. Most impressively, she was the number-one goalie at the 2009 WWC at which she was named the best goalie by the IIHF directorate at tournament's end. Labonte didn't see any ice time at her first Olympics in 2002, was the winning goalie in 2006, and has now, in 2010, established herself as equal to the great Kim St. Pierre.

			GP	W-T-L	Mins	GA	SO	GAA	A	Pim	Place
INTERNATIONAL STATISTICS											
2005	WWC	CAN	2	2-0-0	120:00	0	2	0.00	1	0	S
2006	OG-W	CAN	3	3-0-0	180:00	1	2	0.33	0	0	G
2007	WWC	CAN	2	2-0-0	130:00	4	1	1.85	0	0	G
2008	WWC	CAN	3	1-0-1	138:29	3	1	1.30	0	0	S
2009	WWC	CAN	3	2-0-1	179:04	5	0	1.68	0	0	S

~IIHF Directorate World Women's Championship best goalie (2009)

MACLEOD, CARLA

EDMONTON, ALBERTA,
JUNE 16, 1982

DEFENCE

SHOOTS RIGHT

5'4" 133 LBS

CLUB TEAM: CALGARY OVAL X-TREME, WWHL

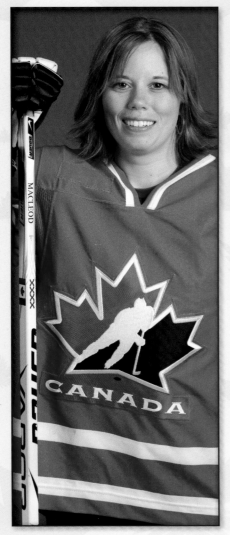

Carla MacLeod graduated from the national U22 women's team to the senior team after playing for the U22 team from 1999 to 2003. She played in the 4 Nations Cup tournaments in 2003 and 2004 and then made her senior debut at the 2005 World Women's Championship, winning a silver medal after a disappointing 1–0 loss in the gold-medal game shootout with the US. Incredibly, Canada did not give up a goal the entire tournament until that shootout.

Her early successes also included victories at the National Women's Championships in 1998 and 2001 with Team Alberta, for which she had played since 1995. She also graduated form the University of Wisconsin in 2005, after serving as captain her final two years, earning a degree in legal studies. She also won the prestigious Medal of Honour at U of W for her combined excellence in athletics and academics.

Since that first WWC in 2005, MacLeod has earned a place on the national team every year, and 2010 in Vancouver marked her second trip to the Olympics. She had an outstanding tournament at last year's WWC, where she was named the best defenceman by the IIHF directorate even though Canada had to settle for silver.

In addition to her performance with the national team, MacLeod has played for the Calgary Oval X-Treme in the WWHL for several years now, helping them to a championship in 2007.

INTERNATIONAL STATISTICS		GP	G	A	P	Pim	Place
2005 WWC	CAN	5	1	2	3	0	S
2006 OG-W	CAN	5	2	2	4	2	G
2007 WWC	CAN	5	0	1	1	2	G
2008 WWC	CAN	5	1	3	4	2	S
2009 WWC	CAN	5	2	6	8	4	S

~IIHF World Women's Championship MVP (2009), World Women's Championship All-Star team/Defence (2006, 2009)

MIKKELSON, MEAGHAN

ST. ALBERT, ALBERTA,
JANUARY 4, 1985

DEFENCE

SHOOTS RIGHT

5'9" 150 LBS

CLUB
TEAM: EDMONTON CHIMOS, WWHL

Meaghan Mikkelson comes from a hockey family. Her father, Bill, played in the NHL in the early 1970s, while her brother, Brendan, won the Memorial Cup in 2007 with the Vancouver Giants and was drafted by Anaheim two years earlier.

In 2002–03, Mikkelson played with the Calgary Oval X-Treme in the NWHL and helped the team win the league championship as well as the national title. Beginning in 2003, Mikkelson played extensively with the national U22 team, winning gold medals at the Air Canada Cup in Germany in 2004, 2005, and 2006.

In 2003, she enrolled at the University of Wisconsin for a four-year program. These were important years for her because midway through she moved from forward back to defence, where she played more naturally. The Badgers went on to win the NCAA Frozen Four both this year and next, Mikkelson's final season in US college hockey. She led all defencemen in scoring this senior year and, after graduation, moved back west to play for the Edmonton Chimos of the WWHL, where she has been ever since.

INTERNATIONAL STATISTICS							
			GP	G	A	P	Pim	Place
2008 WWC	CAN	5	0	0	0	2	S
2009 WWC	CAN	5	0	3	3	6	S

OUELLETTE, CAROLINE

MONTREAL, QUEBEC, MAY 25, 1979

FORWARD

SHOOTS LEFT

5'11" 172 LBS

CLUB TEAM: **MONTREAL STARS, CWHL**

CANADA

If the IIHF had a Triple Gold Club for women, Caroline Ouellette would be one of the founding members. Not only has she won a Gold medal at the Olympics (two, in fact) and World Women's Championship (four in total), she led the Montreal Stars to victory at the inaugural Clarkson Cup in 2009, symbolic of professional supremacy in Canada and similar to the Stanley Cup for women.

Over and above this, Ouellette has led a varied and successful life to date. She played for Quebec at the 1995 Canada Winter Games, and won a gold medal at the national U18 championship in 1997. She won gold with Team Quebec at the nationals in 1999 and 2001, and had a sparkling career at the University of Minnesota-Duluth, all the while playing for the U22 team whenever possible.

Not only did she graduate from UMD with a degree in criminology and women's studies, she won the NCAA championship in 2003 with the Bulldogs and was named MVP of the Final Four tournament. In her senior year, 2005, she was a finalist for the Patty Kazmaier Award for top female player in NCAA hockey, and she was later an assistant coach with the program (2006–08). In her last year, the Bulldogs won another NCAA title. More recently, she has played in the WWHL, although her finest career moments have come with the National Team.

Ouellette has played at every tournament since 1999 (except in 2003 when the WWC was cancelled because of SARS). Along the way she has won gold or silver every year and established herself as a consistent and reliable forward. Not flashy, nor a game-breaker, she is nonetheless the kind of player needed to win championships.

In 2000, Ouellette graduated from the National Police Academy in Quebec.

INTERNATIONAL STATISTICS							
		GP	G	A	P	Pim	Place
1999 WWC	CAN	5	2	5	7	4	G
2000 WWC	CAN	5	0	2	2	2	G
2001 WWC	CAN	5	2	3	5	4	G
2002 OG-W	CAN	5	2	4	6	6	G
2004 WWC	CAN	5	3	6	9	0	G
2005 WWC	CAN	5	2	6	8	0	S
2006 OG-W	CAN	5	5	4	9	4	G
2007 WWC	CAN	5	1	3	4	2	G
2008 WWC	CAN	5	2	4	6	4	S
2009 WWC	CAN	5	3	5	8	6	S

PIPER, CHERIE

TORONTO, ONTARIO,
JUNE 29, 1981

FORWARD

SHOOTS RIGHT

5'6" 167 LBS

CLUB TEAM: CALGARY OVAL X-TREME, WWHL

Like many players, Cherie Piper used Hockey Canada's U22 program as a stepping stone to the senior team and the Olympics. She started with the U22 program playing from 1999–2001, participating in several exhibition games and tournaments, notably 4 Nations Cups in Germany and Switzerland.

Piper had played with Team Ontario as far back as 1997 at the national U18 championship when she was just 16 years old, and played at the Canada Winter Games in 1999. By 2000, she was with the Team Ontario senior team and helped it win a national title.

Starting in 1999, Piper also played in the NWHL but in 2003 she enrolled at Dartmouth College where she also played hockey for the full four years of her program. After graduating in 2007, she returned to pro hockey in Canada, first with the Mississauga Chiefs in the CWHL. It was her goal in the second overtime of the finals that gave the Chiefs a 3–2 win over Brampton to claim the national championship. The next year, she moved out west to play for Calgary in the WWHL.

Piper has been with the senior team since 2002, and has won only gold or silver at the five senior events in which she's competed, most important of which have been the two Gold-medal teams at the 2002 and 2006 Olympics.

INTERNATIONAL STATISTICS							
		GP	G	A	P	Pim	Place
2002 OG-W	CAN	5	3	2	5	0	G
2004 WWC	CAN	5	1	6	7	4	G
2005 WWC	CAN	5	3	1	4	2	S
2006 OG-W	CAN	5	7	8	15	0	G
2008 WWC	CAN	5	2	6	8	0	S

POULIN, MARIE-PHILIP

BEAUCEVILLE, QUEBEC,
MARCH 28, 1991

FORWARD

SHOOTS LEFT

5'6" 160 LBS

CLUB TEAM: DAWSON COLLEGE, CEGEP

The first player to graduate from the newly-created World U18 Championship to play at the Olympics for Canada, Marie-Philip Poulin has demonstrated her scoring ability at every level at which she's played.

Prior to her first U18 in 2008, she played for Team Quebec at the national U18 championships in 2005 and 2007, and was named the best forward at the latter event. She also played for Quebec at the 2007 Canada Winter Games.

Poulin joined the Montreal Stars in the CWHL in 2007–08 and was named rookie of the year. Two years later, she helped the team win the inaugural Clarkson Cup with Team Canada teammates Caroline Ouellette and goalie Kim St. Pierre. She made her Team Canada debut with the U18 team in 2008 at just 16, and tied for the tournament lead in scoring.

She was named best forward by the IIHF directorate, and the next year was almost as impressive for her. Both years she won a silver medal, and this paved the way for her debut with the senior team just a few weeks after her appearance at the 2009 U18. Again, she won silver, and now, at age 18, she is the youngest player on Team Canada's Vancouver roster.

INTERNATIONAL STATISTICS							
		GP	G	A	P	Pim	Place
2008 U18-W	CAN	5	8	6	14	4	S
2009 U18-W	CAN	5	5	7	12	2	S
2009 WWC	CAN	5	2	3	5	0	S

SOSTORICS, COLLEEN

REGINA, SASKATCHEWAN,
DECEMBER 17, 1979

DEFENCE

SHOOTS RIGHT

5'4" 168 LBS

CLUB
TEAM: CALGARY OVAL X-TREME, WWHL

Not one to limit herself, Colleen Sostorics is also an accomplished rugby and fastball player in addition to being one of Canada's pre-eminent hockey players. Indeed, she won the national rugby championship with Team Alberta in 2003, and in her teens won many accolades in fastball.

Sostorics began playing serious hockey in 1995 with Team Saskatchewan at the Canada Winter Games. She had been playing with a boys team in Kennedy, Saskatchewan, her hometown, because there were no girls teams in her rural community. Two years later, she was participating in the national U18 championship, and between 1998 and 2000, she won gold, silver, and bronze at the National Women's Championship. She is also a veteran of the Western Women's Hockey League (WWHL), having played for the Calgary X-Treme since 1999.

Outside of the pro league, Sostorcis won gold medals with Team Alberta at the national championships in 2001, 2003, and 2007. In 2000—01, she was captain of the national U22 team which played in various tournaments around the world. It was her play that year that led to her being named to Canada's team for the 2001 World Women's Championship, her first senior event. Canada won gold, and she has been with the team ever since.

Sostorics has always held education as an important part of her life, and she enrolled at the University of Calgary in 1997, eventually earning her BA in economics in 2004, despite her burgeoning, and time-consuming, career in hockey.

INTERNATIONAL STATISTICS			GP	G	A	P	Pim	Place
2001 WWC	CAN		5	2	1	3	2	G
2002 OG-W	CAN		5	0	2	2	4	G
2004 WWC	CAN		5	1	1	2	2	G
2005 WWC	CAN		5	0	0	0	4	S
2006 OG-W	CAN		5	0	1	1	6	G
2007 WWC	CAN		5	0	3	3	2	G
2008 WWC	CAN		5	0	2	2	10	S
2009 WWC	CAN		5	1	1	2	2	S

ST. PIERRE, KIM

LASALLE, QUEBEC,
DECEMBER 14, 1978

GOALIE

CATCHES LEFT

5'9" 156 LBS

CLUB
TEAM: **MONTREAL STARS, CWHL**

The all-time leader in every important category in international hockey, Kim St. Pierre is the very embodiment of success. Over her ten-year career with Team Canada at the top level, she has played 28 games and recorded a shutout in 15 of them—a record. Her 24 career victories is also a record, and her 0.84 goals-against average is tops for such an extended career.

St. Pierre rose to prominence with Team Quebec, playing at the national championships every year from 1999 to 2001 and being named tournament MVP in the last year. She started a lengthy career with McGill University in 1998 and was named top rookie at season's end. She later played for McGill from 2000 to 2004, earning many honours. She was named MVP at the CIAU championships in 2001, and in 2002–03 was named CIS's most outstanding player. On October 3, 2003, St. Pierre became just the second woman to play in a CIS game when she started for the McGill Redmen in a 4–2 loss to St. Mary's University. Soon after, she became the first woman to win a CIS game when McGill defeated Ryerson University.

After leaving McGill, St. Pierre played in the CWHL, first with the Quebec Avalanche and later with the Montreal Stars. She became an unofficial member of the women's version of the Triple Gold Club by winning the Clarkson Cup in 2009 (along with Caroline Ouellette) having won gold medals at the Olympics (twice) and World Women's Championship (five times). Additionally, she has been named best goalie at three top events, no mean feat given that she often faces only a few shots a game until the semifinals.

			GP	W-T-L	Mins	GA	SO	GAA	A	Pim	Place
					**INTERNATIONAL STATISTICS**						
1999	WWC	CAN	2	2-0-0	120:00	1	1	0.50	0	0	G
2000	WWC	CAN	2	2-0-0	149:58	3	0	1.20	0	0	G
2001	WWC	CAN	3	3-0-0	180:00	2	2	0.67	0	0	G
2002	OG-W	CAN	4	4-0-0	240:00	5	2	1.25	1	0	G
2004	WWC	CAN	4	2-0-1	179:44	3	2	1.00	0	0	G
2005	WWC	CAN	3	2-0-1	200:00	0	3	0.00	0	0	S
2006	OG-W	CAN	2	2-0-0	120:00	1	1	0.50	0	0	G
2007	WWC	CAN	3	3-0-0	180:00	1	2	0.33	0	0	G
2008	WWC	CAN	3	2-0-1	160:00	7	0	2.63	0	0	S
2009	WWC	CAN	2	2-0-0	120:00	0	2	0.00	0	0	S

~IIHF Directorate Olympics best goalie (2002), IIHF Directorate World Women's Championship best goalie (2001, 2004), Olympics All-Star team/Goal (2002), World Women's Championship All-Star team/Goal (2007)

SZABADOS, SHANNON

**EDMONTON, ALBERTA,
AUGUST 6, 1986**

GOALIE

CATCHES LEFT

5'8" 147 LBS

CLUB TEAM: GRANT MACEWAN/ACAC

Although Shannon Szabados has no statistics at the senior level for Team Canada, she is far from inexperienced. As a kid, she played on the same team as Dion Phaneuf, and she later played for several years with the national U22 team. Between 2006 and 2009, Szabados played at the Air Canada Cup three times as well as two exhibition series against the United States.

Trying to crack a goaltending position dominated by Kim St. Pierre and Charline Labonte has been incredibly difficult for the 23-year-old Szabados, but she was named third goalie at the 2009 and 2009 World Women's Championship.

In 2002, at age 16, Szabados became the first female to play junior in the Western Hockey League. She appeared in four exhibition games and one regular-season game (albeit just 20 seconds) with the Tri-City Americans. She then went on to play in the Alberta Junior Hockey League where she won numerous accolades for her play, including top goalie in 2006-07 with Fort Saskatchewan.

Szabados then enrolled at Grant MacEwan College in 2007 and played for the men's team in the Alberta College Athletics Conference.

INTERNATIONAL STATISTICS
no previous experience at WWC or OG

VAILLANCOURT, SARAH

**FLEURIMONT, QUEBEC,
MAY 8, 1985**

FORWARD

SHOOTS RIGHT

5'6" 140 LBS

CLUB TEAM: HARVARD UNIVERSITY, ECAC

Sarah Vaillancourt blossomed while playing with the U22 program starting in 2003, a career that culminated in 2007 when she captained the team to victory at the Air Canada Cup in Germany. She has been a determined and patient player in the senior national team program as well, starting with an appearance in the 4 Nations Cup in Sweden in 2003. A year later, she was an alternate for the 2004 World Women's Championship, and a year after that she was in the lineup.

In fact, her first game at the 2005 WWC came against Kazakhstan, and Vaillancourt had two goals and four assists. Like some NHL players, Vaillancourt used a US prep school as a springboard to greater success. In her case, she attended Pomfret Prep School in Connecticut from 2002 to 2004, and out of this experience she was able to move directly to Harvard University. She was team captain of Pomfret, and in 2003 she captained Team Quebec to a silver medal at the Canada Winter Games.

In her first year at Harvard, Vaillancourt helped the team reach the championship game of the Frozen Four, and she was named rookie of the year for both Ivy League and ECAC. A year later, she was nominated for the Patty Kazmaier Award, and in her third season she won the honour as the NCAA's best female player. Again, in her final year, she was a Kazmaier nominee and was a co-winner for athlete of the year at Harvard.

By the time she graduated, Vaillancourt was considered one of the best hockey players in Harvard history. She has been with the centralized Team Canada for 2009–10 and made the team for Vancouver based on her scoring, experience, and speed.

INTERNATIONAL STATISTICS							
			GP	G	A	P	Pim	Place
2005 WWC	CAN	5	3	5	8	2	S
2006 OG-W	CAN	5	2	4	6	2	G
2007 WWC	CAN	5	2	4	6	4	G
2008 WWC	CAN	5	4	2	6	8	S
2009 WWC	CAN	5	3	4	7	8	S

WARD, CATHERINE

MT. ROYAL, QUEBEC, FEBRUARY 27, 1987

DEFENCE

SHOOTS LEFT

5'6" 135 LBS

CLUB TEAM: **MCGILL UNIVERSITY, CIS**

A major in marketing and international business management at McGill University in Montreal, Catherine Ward is one of the least experienced players on the team. She had been with the U22 national team since 2006, participating in major events including the Fall Festival in 2007, and three MLP/Air Canada Cup events in Germany (2007–09), as well as various exhibition games against, principally, the United States.

Ward began playing serious hockey for Team Quebec at the 2003 Canada Winter Games. She started her career at McGill in 2006, and at season's end was named CIS rookie of the year. The next season, she led McGill to a CIS national championship, and the year after the team successfully defended its title. Ward was named tournament MVP in 2009, and was included in the All-Star team as well.

INTERNATIONAL STATISTICS		GP	G	A	P	Pim	Place
2009 WWC	CAN	5	0	4	4	2	S

WICKENHEISER, HAYLEY

SHAUNAVON, SASKATCHEWAN,
AUGUST 12, 1978

FORWARD

SHOOTS RIGHT

5'10" 171 LBS

CLUB TEAM: EKILSTUNA LINDEN, MEN'S 3RD DIVISION, SWEDEN

CANADA

If anyone deserves the epithet "greatest female hockey player of all time," it is surely Hayley Wickenheiser—pioneer, hero, legend, all-time leader in goals, assists, and points in IIHF women's hockey. From the time she burst on the scene at the 1994 World Women's Championship at the age of 15, right through the 2010 Olympics which she captained, she has accomplished everything a hockey player can possibly aspire to. Indeed, she has played at every tournament for Canada in the last 16 years except for the 2001 World Women's Championship which she missed because of a knee injury.

Such was her reputation and skill, that Philadelphia Flyers general manager Bobby Clarke invited her to participate at the Flyers' rookie camp in 1998 and 1999. On January 31, 2003, she became the first player to score a goal in a senior men's league while playing for HC Salamat, a Division II team in Finland. Wickenheiser played for Salamat in the first half the following season as well, and played with men again in 2008–09 in Sweden.

In 2007, Wickenheiser won the Bobbie Rosenfeld Award as the female athlete of the year as selected by Canadian Press. She is known for being the complete player, one without flaw. Her skating stride is powerful, her shot of near-NHL calibre. Her leadership is unquestioned, and her passing pinpoint. There is nothing she can't do on the ice.

She has been named MVP of the women's nationals on six occasions, and during her four years with the Calgary Oval X-Treme in the WWHL, led the team to the championship three times.

In all, she has won Olympic Gold twice and silver once, and World Women's Championship gold six times and silver three times. She has been named tournament MVP a record three times and best forward by the IIHF directorate four times, another record.

INTERNATIONAL STATISTICS			GP	G	A	P	Pim	Place
1994 WWC	CAN		3	0	1	1	4	G
1997 WWC	CAN		5	4	5	9	12	G
1998 OG-W	CAN		6	2	6	8	4	S
1999 WWC	CAN		5	3	5	8	8	G
2000 WWC	CAN		5	1	7	8	4	G
2002 OG-W	CAN		5	7	3	10	2	G
2004 WWC	CAN		5	3	2	5	2	G
2005 WWC	CAN		5	5	3	8	6	S
2006 OG-W	CAN		5	5	12	17	6	G
2007 WWC	CAN		5	8	6	14	0	G
2008 WWC	CAN		5	3	6	9	6	S
2009 WWC	CAN		5	4	4	8	4	S

~ IIHF Tournament MVP (2002, 2006, 2007), IIHF Directorate Olympics best forward (2002, 2006), IIHF Directorate World Women's Championship best forward (2007, 2009), Olympics All-Star team/Forward (2002, 2006), World Women's Championship All-Star team/Forward (1997, 1999, 2005, 2007, 2008)

MEN'S FINAL STANDINGS

Final Placings

Gold Medal	Canada
Silver Medal	United States
Bronze Medal	Finland
Fourth Place	Slovakia
Fifth Place	Sweden
Sixth Place	Russia
Seventh Place	Czech Republic
Eighth Place	Switzerland
Ninth Place	Belarus
Tenth Place	Norway
Eleventh Place	Germany
Twelfth Place	Latvia

Directorate Awards

Best Goalie
Ryan Miller (USA)
Best Defenceman
Brian Rafalski (USA)
Best Forward
Jonathan Toews (CAN)

All-Star Team

Goal: Ryan Miller (USA)
Defence: Shea Weber (CAN)
Brian Rafalski (USA)
Forward: Jonathan Toews (CAN)
Pavol Demitra (SVK)
Zach Parise (USA)

Tournament MVP
Ryan Miller (USA)

Final Standings

Group A

	GP	W	OTW	OTL	L	GF	GA	P
United States	3	3	0	0	0	14	5	9
Canada	3	1	1	0	1	14	7	5
Switzerland	3	0	1	1	1	8	10	3
Norway	3	0	0	1	2	5	19	1

February 16	**United States 3 — Switzerland 1**	February 18	**Canada 3 — Switzerland 2 (SO)**
February 16	**Canada 8 — Norway 0**	February 20	**Switzerland 5 — Norway 4 (OT)**
February 18	**United States 6 — Norway 1**	February 21	**United States 5 — Canada 3**

Group B

	GP	W	OTW	OTL	L	GF	GA	P
Russia	3	2	0	1	0	13	6	7
Czech Republic	3	2	0	0	1	10	7	6
Slovakia	3	1	1	0	1	9	4	5
Latvia	3	0	0	0	3	4	19	0

February 16	**Russia 8 — Latvia 2**	February 19	**Czech Republic 5 — Latvia 2**
February 17	**Czech Republic 3 — Slovakia 1**	February 20	**Slovakia 6 — Latvia 0**
February 18	**Slovakia 2 — Russia 1 (SO)**	February 21	**Russia 4 — Czech Republic 2**

Final Standings

Group C

	GP	W	OTW	OTL	L	GF	GA	P
Sweden	3	3	0	0	0	9	2	9
Finland	3	2	0	0	1	10	4	6
Belarus	3	1	0	0	2	8	12	3
Germany	3	0	0	0	3	3	12	0

February 17	**Finland** 5 — Belarus 1	February 19	**Finland** 5 — Germany 0
February 17	**Sweden** 2 — Germany 0	February 20	**Belarus** 5 — Germany 3
February 19	**Sweden** 4 — Belarus 2	February 21	**Sweden** 3 — Finland 0

Qualification Playoff

February 23	**Switzerland** 3 — Belarus 2	February 23	**Czech Republic** 3 — Latvia 2 (OT)
February 23	**Canada** 8 — Germany 2	February 23	**Slovakia** 4 — Norway 3

Quarter-finals

February 24	**United States** 2 — Switzerland 0	February 24	**Finland** 2 — Czech Republic 0
February 24	**Canada** 7 — Russia 3	February 24	**Slovakia** 4 — Sweden 3

Semifinals

February 26	**United States** 6 — Finland 1
February 26	**Canada** 3 — Slovakia 2

Bronze-Medal Game

February 27	**Finland** 5 — Slovakia 3

Gold-Medal Game

February 28	**Canada** 3 — United States 2 (OT)

WOMEN'S FINAL STANDINGS

Final Placings

Gold Medal	Canada
Silver Medal	United States
Bronze Medal	Finland
Fourth Place	Sweden
Fifth Place	Switzerland
Sixth Place	Russia
Seventh Place	China
Eighth Place	Slovakia

Directorate Awards

Best Goalie
   Shannon Szabados (CAN)
Best Defenceman
   Molly Engstrom (USA)
Best Forward
   Meghan Agosta (CAN)

All-Star Team

Goal: Shannon Szabados (CAN)
Defence: Angela Ruggiero (USA)
   Molly Engstrom (USA)
Forward: Meghan Agosta (CAN)
   Jenny Potter (USA)
   Marie-Philip Poulin (CAN)

Tournament MVP
Meghan Agosta (CAN)

Final Standings

Group A

	GP	W	OTW	OTL	L	GF	GA	P
Canada	3	3	0	0	0	41	2	9
Sweden	3	2	0	0	1	10	15	6
Switzerland	3	1	0	0	2	6	15	3
Slovakia	3	0	0	0	3	4	29	0

February 13	Sweden 3 — Switzerland 0	February 15	Sweden 6 — Slovakia 2
February 13	Canada 18 — Slovakia 0	February 17	Canada 13 — Sweden 1
February 15	Canada 10 — Switzerland 1	February 17	Switzerland 5 — Slovakia 2

Group B

	GP	W	OTW	OTL	L	GF	GA	P
United States	3	3	0	0	0	31	1	9
Finland	3	2	0	0	1	7	8	6
Russia	3	1	0	0	2	3	19	3
China	3	0	0	0	3	3	16	0

February 14	United States 12 — China 1	February 16	Finland 2 — China 1
February 14	Finland 5 — Russia 1	February 18	United States 6 — Finland 0
February 16	United States 13 — Russia 0	February 18	Russia 2 — China 1

Placement Games

February 20	Switzerland 6 — China 0	February 22	China 3 — Slovakia 1
February 20	Russia 4 — Slovakia 2	February 22	Switzerland 2 — Russia 1 (SO)

Semifinals

February 22	United States 9 — Sweden 1
February 22	Canada 5 — Finland 0

Bronze-Medal Game

February 25	Finland 3 — Sweden 2 (OT)

Gold-Medal Game

February 25	Canada 2 — United States 0

FINAL STATISTICS—MEN

Belarus

	GP	G	A	P	Pim
Sergei Kostitsyn	4	2	3	5	0
Aleksei Kalyuzhny	4	3	1	4	2
Nikolai Stasenko	4	0	3	3	2
Dmitri Meleshko	4	2	0	2	2
Aleksei Ugarov	4	1	1	2	4
Konstantin Koltsov	4	0	2	2	0
Konstantin Zakharov	4	1	0	1	4
Ruslan Salei	4	1	0	1	0
Sergei Demagin	4	0	1	1	2
Viktor Kostiuchenok	4	0	1	1	2
Aleksandr Ryadinski	4	0	1	1	2
Aleksandr Kulakov	4	0	1	1	0
Aleksandr Makritski	4	0	0	0	4
Andrei Karev	4	0	0	0	2
Andrei Mikhalev	4	0	0	0	2
Andrei Stas	4	0	0	0	2
Oleg Antonenko	4	0	0	0	0
Vladimir Denisov	4	0	0	0	0
Sergei Kolosov	4	0	0	0	0
Sergei Zadelenov	4	0	0	0	0
Vitali Koval	2	0	0	0	0
Andrei Mezin	2	0	0	0	0

In Goal	GP	W-L	Mins	GA	SO	GAA
Vitali Koval	2	1-1	120:00	8	0	4.00
Andrei Mezin	2	0-2	130:00	7	0	3.23

Canada

	GP	G	A	P	Pim
Jonathan Toews	7	1	7	8	2
Jarome Iginla	7	5	2	7	0
Sidney Crosby	7	4	3	7	4
Dany Heatley	7	4	3	7	4
Ryan Getzlaf	7	3	4	7	2
Shea Weber	7	2	4	6	2
Eric Staal	7	1	5	6	6
Dan Boyle	7	1	5	6	2
Duncan Keith	7	0	6	6	2
Corey Perry	7	4	1	5	2
Rick Nash	7	2	3	5	0
Mike Richards	7	2	3	5	0
Patrick Marleau	7	2	3	5	0
Chris Pronger	7	0	5	5	2
Brenden Morrow	7	2	1	3	2
Scott Niedermayer	7	1	2	3	4
Joe Thornton	7	1	1	2	0
Drew Doughty	7	0	2	2	2
Patrice Bergeron	7	0	1	1	2
Brent Seabrook	7	0	1	1	2
Martin Brodeur	2	0	0	0	0
Roberto Luongo	5	0	0	0	0

In Goal	GP	W-T-L	Mins	GA	SO	GAA
Martin Brodeur	2	1-1	124:18	6	0	2.90
Roberto Luongo	5	5-0	307:40	9	1	1.76

Czech Republic

	GP	G	A	P	Pim
Marek Zidlicky	5	0	5	5	2
Patrik Elias	5	2	2	4	2
Jaromir Jagr	5	2	1	3	6
David Krejci	5	2	1	3	6
Tomas Plekanec	5	2	1	3	2
Tomas Fleischmann	5	1	2	3	2
Tomas Kaberle	5	1	2	3	0
Milan Michalek	5	2	0	2	2
Miroslav Blatak	5	0	2	2	2
Roman Cervenka	5	0	2	2	0
Martin Havlat	5	0	2	2	0
Tomas Rolinek	5	1	0	1	0
Martin Erat	5	0	1	1	2
Filip Kuba	5	0	1	1	0
Petr Cajanek	5	0	0	0	6
Jan Hejda	5	0	0	0	4
Roman Polak	5	0	0	0	4
Zbynek Michalek	5	0	0	0	2
Pavel Kubina	5	0	0	0	2
Josef Vasicek	5	0	0	0	2
Tomas Vokoun	5	0	0	0	0

In Goal	GP	W-L	Mins	GA	SO	GAA
Tomas Vokoun	5	3-2	303:35	9	0	1.78

Finland

	GP	G	A	P	Pim
Lasse Kukkonen	6	0	1	1	4
Sami Salo	6	1	1	2	4
Teemu Selanne	6	0	2	2	0
Mikko Koivu	6	0	4	4	2
Niklas Hagman	6	4	2	6	2
Saku Koivu	6	0	2	2	6
Olli Jokinen	6	3	1	4	2
Tuomu Ruutu	6	1	0	1	2
Ville Peltonen	6	0	1	1	2
Sami Lepisto	6	0	1	1	6
Antti Miettinen	6	1	0	1	0
Janne Niskala	6	0	2	2	2
Joni Pitkanen	5	1	2	3	29
Jere Lehtinen	6	0	0	0	0
Toni Lydman	6	0	0	0	2
Niklas Backstrom	6	0	0	0	2
Miikka Kiprusoff	6	0	1	1	0
Jarkko Ruutu	6	2	1	3	14
Niko Kapanen	6	0	2	2	0
Kimmo Timonen	6	2	2	4	2
Valtteri Filppula	6	3	0	3	0
Jarkko Immonen	6	0	0	0	0

In Goal	GP	W-T-L	Mins	GA	SO	GAA
Niklas Backstrom	2	1-0	109:52	2	1	1.09
Miikka Kiprusoff	5	3-2	350:08	11	1	2.64

Germany

	GP	G	A	P	Pim
Marcel Goc	4	2	1	3	0
Marcel Muller	4	0	2	2	12
Dennis Seidenberg	4	1	0	1	2
John Tripp	4	1	0	1	2
Manuel Klinge	4	1	0	1	0
Jochen Hecht	4	0	1	1	2
Kai Hospelt	4	0	1	1	2
Chris Schmidt	4	0	1	1	2
Andre Rankel	4	0	1	1	0
Marco Sturm	4	0	1	1	0
Christian Ehrhoff	4	0	0	0	4
Jakub Ficenec	4	0	0	0	4
Alexander Sulzer	4	0	0	0	4
Sven Butenschon	4	0	0	0	2
Sven Felski	4	0	0	0	2
Thomas Greilinger	4	0	0	0	2
Korbinian Holzer	4	0	0	0	2
Travis Mulock	4	0	0	0	2
Michael Wolf	4	0	0	0	2
Michael Bakos	4	0	0	0	0
Thomas Greiss	3	0	0	0	0
Dmitri Patzold	1	0	0	0	0

In Goal	GP	W-L	Mins	GA	SO	GAA
Thomas Greiss	3	0-3	178:51	15	0	5.03
Dmitri Patzold	1	0-1	60:00	5	0	5.00

Latvia

	GP	G	A	P	Pim
Girts Ankipans	4	2	0	2	4
Herberts Vasiljevs	4	1	1	2	6
Martins Cipulis	4	1	1	2	0
Martins Karsums	4	0	2	2	2
Aleksandrs Nizivijs	4	0	2	2	2
Mikelis Redlihs	4	1	0	1	4
Lauris Darzins	4	0	1	1	10
Kristaps Sotnieks	4	0	1	1	4
Armands Berzins	4	0	1	1	2
Georgijs Pujacs	4	0	1	1	2
Krisjanis Redlihs	4	0	1	1	2
Janis Sprukts	4	0	1	1	0
Arvids Rekis	4	0	0	0	10
Oskars Bartulis	4	0	0	0	2
Kaspara Daugavins	4	0	0	0	2
Gints Meija	4	0	0	0	2
Aleksejs Sirokovs	4	0	0	0	2
Guntis Galvins	2	0	0	0	0
Rodrigo Lavins	4	0	0	0	0
Edgars Masalskis	4	0	0	0	0
Karlis Skrastins	4	0	0	0	0

In Goal	GP	W-L	Mins	GA	SO	GAA
Edgars Masalskis	4	0-4	244:35	21	0	5.15

Norway

	GP	G	A	P	Pim
Patrick Thoresen	4	0	5	5	0
Tore Vikingstad	4	4	0	4	4
Mathis Olimb	4	0	2	2	0
Anders Bastiansen	4	1	0	1	4
Mads Hansen	4	1	0	1	2
Marius Holtet	4	1	0	1	0
Tommy Jakobsen	4	0	1	1	8
Jonas Holos	4	0	1	1	2
Ole Kristian Tollefsen	3	0	0	0	25
Alexander Bonsaksen	4	0	0	0	2
Lars Erik Spets	4	0	0	0	2
Mats Trygg	4	0	0	0	2
Jonas Andersen	4	0	0	0	0
Kristian Forsberg	4	0	0	0	0
Pal Grotnes	4	0	0	0	0
Juha Kaunismaki	4	0	0	0	0
Martin Laumann Ylven	4	0	0	0	0
Lars Erik Lund	4	0	0	0	0
Martin Roymark	4	0	0	0	0
Andre Lysenstoen	1	0	0	0	0
Per-Age Skroder	1	0	0	0	0

In Goal	GP	W-L	Mins	GA	SO	GAA
Pal Grotnes	4	0-4	226:11	19	0	5.04
Andre Lysenstoen	1	0-0	15:31	4	0	15.47

Russia

	GP	G	A	P	Pim
Evgeni Malkin	4	3	3	6	0
Alexander Ovechkin	4	2	2	4	2
Sergei Fedorov	4	0	4	4	6
Pavel Datsyuk	4	1	2	3	2
Ilya Kovalchuk	4	1	2	3	0
Danis Zaripov	4	2	0	2	2
Alexei Morozov	4	2	0	2	0
Alexander Radulov	4	1	1	2	4
Maxim Afinogenov	4	1	1	2	0
Dmitri Kalinin	4	1	1	2	0
Alexander Semin	4	0	2	2	4
Fedor Tyutin	4	0	2	2	2
Andrei Markov	4	0	2	2	0
Sergei Zinoviev	4	0	2	2	0
Sergei Gonchar	4	1	0	1	2
Viktor Kozlov	4	1	0	1	0
Denis Grebeshkov	4	0	1	1	2
Ilya Nikulin	4	0	1	1	2
Anton Volchenkov	4	0	1	1	2
Konstantin Korneyev	4	0	0	0	4
Evgeni Nabokov	3	0	0	0	0
Ilya Bryzgalov	2	0	0	0	0

In Goal	GP	W-L	Mins	GA	SO	GAA
Evgeni Nabokov	3	2-1	144:07	10	0	4.16
Ilya Bryzgalov	2	0-1	100:53	3	0	1.78

Slovakia

	GP	G	A	P	Pim
Ivan Baranka	7	1	0	1	0
Martin Cibak	7	0	0	0	6
Marian Gaborik	7	4	1	5	6
Andrej Meszaros	7	0	0	0	4
Jozef Stumpel	7	1	4	5	0
Lubomir Visnovsky	7	2	1	3	0
Miroslav Satan	6	1	1	2	0
Richard Zednik	7	2	4	6	6
Lubos Bartecko	7	0	1	1	0
Zigmund Palffy	7	0	3	3	8
Michal Handzus	7	3	3	6	0
Zdeno Chara	7	0	3	3	6
Pavol Demitra	7	3	7	10	2
Jaroslav Halak	7	0	0	0	0
Andrej Sekera	7	1	0	1	0
Milan Jurcina	7	0	0	0	2
Martin Strbak	7	0	1	1	2
Marian Hossa	7	3	6	9	6
Tomas Kopecky	7	1	0	1	2
Marcel Hossa	7	0	1	1	0
Branko Radivojevic	7	0	0	0	6

In Goal	GP	W-T-L	Mins	GA	SO	GAA
Jaroslav Halak	7	4-3	422:38	17	1	2.41

Switzerland

	GP	G	A	P	Pim
Severin Blindenbacher	5	1	1	2	4
Mark Streit	5	0	3	3	0
Andres Ambuhl	5	0	0	0	0
Roman Wick	5	2	3	5	2
Rafael Diaz	5	0	0	0	4
Hnat Domenichelli	5	1	2	3	4
Thomas Deruns	5	0	0	0	0
Thierry Paterlini	5	0	1	1	6
Thibaut Monnet	5	0	1	1	0
Martin Pluss	5	0	3	3	0
Mathias Seger	5	0	2	2	4
Ivo Ruthemann	5	1	0	1	0
Sandy Jeannin	5	0	1	1	2
Raffaele Sannitz	5	1	1	2	8
Luca Sbisa	5	0	0	0	0
Philippe Furrer	5	0	1	1	2
Romano Lemm	5	2	0	2	2
Patrick von Gunten	5	1	0	1	0
Yannick Weber	5	0	0	0	6
Julien Sprunger	5	2	0	2	2
Jonas Hiller	5	0	0	0	0

In Goal	GP	W-L	Mins	GA	SO	GAA
Jonas Hiller	5	2-3	315:57	13	0	2.47

Sweden

	GP	G	A	P	Pim
Nicklas Backstrom	4	1	5	6	0
Loui Eriksson	4	3	1	4	0
Daniel Alfredsson	4	3	0	3	0
Daniel Sedin	4	1	2	3	0
Johan Franzen	4	1	1	2	2
Tobias Enstrom	4	0	2	2	4
Magnus Johansson	4	0	2	2	2
Henrik Sedin	4	0	2	2	2
Mattias Weinhandl	4	0	2	2	2
Patric Hornqvist	4	1	0	1	4
Mattias Ohlund	4	1	0	1	2
Henrik Zetterberg	4	1	0	1	2
Peter Forsberg	4	0	1	1	2
Samuel Pahlsson	3	0	1	1	2
Fredrik Modin	3	0	1	1	0
Johnny Oduya	4	0	0	0	12
Henrik Tallinder	4	0	0	0	4
Niklas Kronwall	4	0	0	0	2
Nicklas Lidstrom	4	0	0	0	2
Douglas Murray	4	0	0	0	0
Henrik Lundqvist	3	0	0	0	0
Jonas Gustavsson	1	0	0	0	0

In Goal	GP	W-L	Mins	GA	SO	GAA
Henrik Lundqvist	3	2-1	179:05	4	2	1.34
Jonas Gustavsson	1	1-0	60:00	2	0	2.00

United States

	GP	G	A	P	Pim
Brian Rafalski	6	4	4	8	2
Zach Parise	6	4	4	8	0
Ryan Malone	6	3	2	5	6
Patrick Kane	6	3	2	5	2
Jamie Langenbrunner	6	1	3	4	0
Ryan Suter	6	0	4	4	2
David Backes	6	1	2	3	2
Paul Stastny	6	1	2	3	0
Joe Pavelski	6	0	3	3	4
Ryan Kesler	6	2	0	2	2
Chris Drury	6	2	0	2	0
Bobby Ryan	6	1	1	2	2
Phil Kessel	6	1	1	2	0
Erik Johnson	6	1	0	1	4
Ryan Callahan	6	0	1	1	2
Jack Johnson	6	0	1	1	2
Ryan Miller	6	0	1	1	0
Dustin Brown	6	0	0	0	0
Tim Gleason	6	0	0	0	0
Brooks Orpik	6	0	0	0	0
Ryan Whitney	6	0	0	0	0
Tim Thomas	1	0	0	0	0

In Goal	GP	W-T-L	Mins	GA	SO	GAA
Ryan Miller	6	5-1	355:07	8	1	1.35
Tim Thomas	1	0-0	11:31	1	0	5.21

FINAL STATISTICS—WOMEN

Canada

	GP	G	A	P	Pim
Meghan Agosta	5	9	6	15	2
Jayna Hefford	5	5	7	12	8
Caroline Ouellette	5	2	9	11	2
Hayley Wickenheiser	5	2	9	11	0
Cherie Piper	5	5	5	10	0
Sarah Vaillancourt	5	3	5	8	6
Marie-Philip Poulin	5	5	2	7	2
Gillian Apps	5	3	4	7	2
Rebecca Johnston	5	1	5	6	2
Colleen Sostorics	5	1	5	6	2
Haley Irwin	5	4	1	5	4
Carla MacLeod	5	2	3	5	2
Becky Kellar	5	0	4	4	6
Catherine Ward	5	2	2	4	4
Tessa Bonhomme	5	2	2	4	0
Gina Kingsbury	5	2	1	3	6
Jennifer Botterill	5	0	2	2	0
Meaghan Mikkelson	5	0	0	0	2
Shannon Szabados	3	0	0	0	0
Kim St. Pierre	2	0	0	0	0
Charline Labonte	1	0	0	0	0

In Goal	GP	W-L	Mins	GA	SO	GAA
Shannon Szabados	3	3-0	180:00	1	2	0.33
Charline Labonte	1	0-0	20:00	1	0	3.00
Kim St. Pierre	2	2-0	100:00	0	1	0.00

China

	GP	G	A	P	Pim
Linuo Wang	5	3	0	3	4
Fengling Jin	5	2	1	3	4
Rui Sun	5	1	2	3	0
Na Jiang	5	0	1	1	4
Rui Ma	5	0	1	1	4
Shuang Zhang	5	0	1	1	4
Baiwei Yu	5	0	1	1	2
Ben Zhang	5	0	1	1	2
Xueting Qi	5	0	0	0	6
Haijing Huang	5	0	0	0	4
Zhixin Liu	5	0	0	0	4
Anqi Tan	5	0	0	0	4
Shanshan Cui	5	0	0	0	2
Yue Lou	5	0	0	0	2
Fujin Gao	5	0	0	0	0
Cui Huo	5	0	0	0	0
Yao Shi	5	0	0	0	0
Liang Tang	5	0	0	0	0
Mengying Zhang	5	0	0	0	0
Dandan Jia	1	0	0	0	0

In Goal	GP	W-L	Mins	GA	SO	GAA
Yao Shi	5	1-4	247:53	19	0	4.60
Dandan Jia	1	0-0	52:07	4	0	4.61

Finland

	GP	G	A	P	Pim
Karoliina Rantamaki	5	2	1	3	4
Michelle Karvinen	5	1	2	3	4
Heidi Pelttari	5	1	2	3	4
Venla Hovi	5	2	0	2	2
Nina Tikkinen	5	2	0	2	0
Jenni Hiirikoski	5	0	2	2	4
Linda Valimaki	5	0	2	2	4
Saara Tuominen	5	0	2	2	2
Saija Sirvio	5	1	0	1	4
Marjo Voutilainen	5	1	0	1	4
Rosa Lindstedt	5	0	1	1	10
Mari Saarinen	5	0	1	1	2
Terhi Mertanen	5	0	0	0	6
Emma Laaksonen	5	0	0	0	2
Mariia Posa	5	0	0	0	2
Anne Helin	5	0	0	0	0
Annina Rajahuhta	5	0	0	0	0
Noora Raty	5	0	0	0	0
Minnamari Tuominen	5	0	0	0	0

In Goal	GP	W-L	Mins	GA	SO	GAA
Noora Raty	5	3-2	302:33	15	0	2.97

Russia

	GP	G	A	P	Pim
Marina Sergina	5	1	2	3	8
Tatiana Burina	5	1	2	3	4
Iya Gavrilova	5	2	0	2	6
Ekaterina Smolentseva	5	1	1	2	10
Olga Permyakova	4	0	2	2	10
Alexandra Kapustina	5	0	2	2	2
Tatiana Sotnikova	5	1	0	1	2
Svetlana Terenteva	5	1	0	1	2
Aleksandra Vafina	5	1	0	1	2
Inna Dyubanok	5	0	1	1	4
Ekaterina Lebedeva	5	0	1	1	2
Alena Khomich	5	0	1	1	0
Kristina Petrovskaya	5	0	0	0	4
Olga Sosina	5	0	0	0	2
Svetlana Tkacheva	5	0	0	0	2
Ekaterina Ananina	5	0	0	0	0
Yulia Deulina	5	0	0	0	0
Zoya Polunina	5	0	0	0	0
Irina Gashennikova	4	0	0	0	0
Maria Onolbayva	1	0	0	0	0
Anna Prugova	1	0	0	0	0

In Goal	GP	W-L	Mins	GA	SO	GAA
Anna Prugova	1	0-1	31:00	10	0	19.35
Irina Gashennikova	4	2-2	250:00	10	0	2.40
Maria Onolbayva	1	0-0	29:00	3	0	6.21